# OVARCOMING

Be Inspired

**Copyright © [2024] by [Ovarcome]**

**ISBN:** 979-8-9916222-0-2 (print)

**All rights reserved.**

No part of this publication may be reproduced, distributed, or transmitted in any form or by any means, including photocopying, recording, or other electronic or mechanical methods, without the prior written permission of the publisher, except as permitted by U.S. copyright law. For permission requests, contact [Ovarcome/info@ovarcome.org].

For privacy reasons, some names, locations, and dates may have been changed.

**Book Cover by [Ovarcome]**

1st edition [2024]

# TO OVARCOMERS

Keep inspiring
Keep Ovarcoming

## Finding Light in Ovarcoming

An ovarian cancer diagnosis is life changing. The future seems uncertain, and anxiety can easily take hold. But within the dismay, and the challenges that inevitably follow, we uncover a spark of resilience, a quiet strength waiting to be discovered.

This book isn't a medical guide, but rather a companion on your journey of Ovarcoming. It's a space to explore the importance of laughter in the face of hardship, a reminder that the most valuable things in life can't be measured by a scan.

It's about the love that surrounds us, the connections that sustain us, and the moments of joy that sprinkle sunshine even on the cloudiest days.

Here, you'll meet incredible women who have Ovarcome in their own unique ways.

Their stories will show you the strength that comes from leaning on loved ones, the comfort found in shared experiences, and the power of harnessing hope.

While challenges are difficult, facing them head-on is the only way out. In the process, oftentimes, you discover your heart opening to unexpected beauty. This book explores how shifting our perspective allows us to see possibilities amid challenges. It's about discovering that even the most painful situations can lead to personal growth and a deeper appreciation for life's precious moments.

As you turn the pages, you'll find humor, introspection, and a supportive community. So, take a deep breath, grab a warm beverage, and join us on this journey. Together, we'll explore the power of community through stories of hope and the strength that lies within us all. Remember, you're not alone on this path. Together, we will Ovarcome.

"

If you feel bloated, if you are having pain, and if you have any blood while urinating… go to a doctor who will test you properly… and insist, insist, insist.

*- Theresa Pinola*

# Theresa Pinola

Plagued by an overactive bladder, Theresa had been seeing an urologist for a while and was on medication to ease her discomfort. However, at one point, Theresa developed pain in her side. Upon hearing this, her doctor thought she had a kidney stone. But in the ensuing CAT scan, the doctors discovered a mass in her right ovary. Before getting an official diagnosis, Theresa says she went months going from doctor to doctor and simply debating the next steps with her husband.

"I was a little bloated at the time but then you know I'm 65, not a serious exerciser either. I walk, yes, but I love to eat too. It was the period between Thanksgiving and Christmas because we cook a lot during this time." After the CAT scan and receiving her official ovarian cancer diagnosis, Theresa's doctor did a full hysterectomy on her.

With her procedures complete, three and half weeks later, Theresa began chemo. Before her diagnosis, Theresa had dutifully been going to her gynecologist for her yearly physicals, and she remembers telling her doctor how she was having pain 'down there'. After a specific checkup, she recalls her doctor saying 'Oh, you're fine, it's nothing. You are good.'"

In light of this unfortunate experience, Theresa encourages women to be extra cautious: "If you feel bloated, if you are having pain, and if you have any blood while urinating… go to a doctor who will test you properly… and insist, insist, insist." But despite the surgeries, chemo sessions, and uncertainties that inevitably come along on a cancer journey, Theresa, with her eight grandchildren and two daughters, had found the strength to Ovarcome.

If you find yourself in the valley of life, wear your strongest hiking boots, lift your hands up to grab onto hope and Keep climbing.

"

I believe that hope should be developed, nurtured, and shared. Life can change very quickly. I always found comfort in knowing that God may not take away the situation, but he will give me the power to endure and thrive. I was determined to live joyfully with cancer.

*- Tonya Childress*

# Tonya Childress

## Finding Out

At the time of this writing, Tonya is in recurrence and active treatment. Her journey with cancer first began in 2007 and surgeries took place intermittently every second year for tumor removal.

"Up until the second surgery, the tumors were considered non-cancerous. On my third surgery, the biopsy samples revealed that it was a low-grade serous carcinoma."

"I remember going into a follow up visit after the surgery and I felt calm because it was a routine visit but then I heard the doctor say 'your biopsy was positive for cancer'.

I wouldn't change anything about that day because I had my husband with me.

Since it was a routine follow up I wasn't nervous or anxious because I wasn't anticipating any news, but I took comfort that my best friend, my husband, was with me and I prayed for understanding, direction and for confidence."

Thus began Tonya's journey with ovarian cancer: series of surgeries, chemotherapy, radiation, clinical trial, and ongoing treatment over several years..

## Journey

Through it all, Tonya draws strength from her relationship with God, the unwavering support of her husband and family, and the comforting presence of friends in her congregation. On rough days, Tonya practices positive thinking and finds solace in prayer, seeking strength, comfort, and focus.

She shared, "I believe that hope should be developed, nurtured, and shared. Life can change very quickly. I always found comfort in knowing that God may not take away the situation, but he will give me the power to endure and thrive. I was determined to live joyfully with cancer."

"Always believe in God's power," Tonya emphasizes, acknowledging that while cancer may persist, God provides the strength to endure with love and positivity.

Her message to everyone with ovarian cancer is clear: "Don't give up."

## Ovarcoming

For Tonya, cancer awareness is not just a cause; it's a lifeline. She understands that early detection can significantly impact outcomes.

She plans to amplify awareness by sharing the BEACH symptoms on social media and engaging in conversations about ovarian cancer without hesitation or embarrassment.

"The symptoms mimic so many other gastrointestinal issues. Be safe, not sorry. You know your body better than anyone. Ovarian cancer awareness is important because the sooner you know the signs or see a doctor, the better your outcome can be."

Amidst her journey, Tonya finds solace and strength in the community fostered by Ovarcome.

She recognizes the power in numbers and the importance of women feeling connected, their journey becomes better by the camaraderie of fellow Ovarcomers.

"When you feel connected to others meaningfully, the outcomes are always better."

Tonya Childress, an Ovarcomer in every sense, radiates resilience, spreads hope, and stands as a testament to the power of faith, love, and the unyielding human spirit in the face of adversity.

Her story is an inspiration for all those Ovarcoming.

**Embrace that happy moment.
It empowers you to Ovarcome.**

> **It is a struggle with chemo but keep Ovarcoming one day at a time, every day, and keep moving forward.**
>
> *- Tarah Schreckengaust*

# Tarah Schreckengaust

Struggling from bloating and fluid build-up in her abdomen, Tarah, unable to breathe properly, visited her doctor. Her doctor ordered labs, a CT, and a PET scan, all of which revealed heightened calcium levels and peritoneal carcinoma.

Tarah had been experiencing symptoms for one to two months before she was diagnosed: "I could not breathe and that pushed me to get myself checked even though I had no pain"

Tarah is not new to cancer. Tarah was initially diagnosed with breast cancer. She got her genetic testing done and "everything was negative," she says.

Tarah is blessed with strong social support from her family and friends, who help her around the house and shower her with their love and care. Tarah is looking toward clinical trials - "Just them trying science, new formulations of medications to see if it can help with different types of cancers, I'm positively looking towards them," she says.

Tarah sees strong hope in the emerging breakthroughs in the field of cancer research. Tarah conquers each day at a time, to tell the story. "It's a struggle with chemo but keep Ovarcoming one day at a time, every day, and keep moving forward."

It is by her sheer strength, positivity, and willpower that she has done just that, standing true to the promise of a true Ovarcomer.

**For every mountain, there's the spirit of Ovarcoming. Keep climbing.**

> My life perspective is that each day is a gift. Remember that you are not alone on this journey.
>
> *- Betty White*

# Betty White

## Finding Out

In 1997, I was 45 years old and experiencing symptoms of extreme fatigue and intermittent lower abdominal pain. My gynecologist ran a transvaginal ultrasound which alone did not indicate something serious. He wanted to monitor the pain which continued to escalate. Additionally, I was experiencing extreme constipation. I consulted a GI doctor and had a colonoscopy, which came clear. After 4 months of tests and results, my gynecologist and I chose a laparoscopic procedure which developed into a complete hysterectomy and removal of both ovaries.

## Journey

As I was hospitalized, the next evening after the surgery, pathology called my doctor to reveal ovarian cancer in both ovaries. I was diagnosed with high-grade serous and clear cell, poorly differentiated, stage 1C ovarian cancer. After my second opinion, I began chemotherapy three weeks later.

My initial response was concern for my daughter who was in high school at the time and expecting me home since it was to be a day procedure. My parents had not come from out of town. I waited to hear what the doctors would do for treatment. My response and attitude overall was let's get started so I can start living my life again.

## Ovarcoming

My treatment journey was chemo every three weeks for 6 rounds. In the 4th round, my red blood counts were too low. So I was delayed several weeks, waiting for my blood count to rise.

My husband stayed with me in my room for all 6 treatments. Four months after completing my treatment, I chose a second-look surgery which tested 24 abdominal sites which were all clear. When genetic testing was available, I was tested twice but no known mutations were detected.

My side effects were fatigue, leg pain, and loss of appetite even though the doctor told me to eat everything I wanted, complete hair loss on my entire body after the first treatment, hearing sensitivity, inability to tolerate crowds or activities, neuropathy in my hands and feet and chemo brain. My walking was impaired to the point that I eventually worked with a personal trainer to regain my balance and be able to walk well again. The weakness, neuropathy, and compromised immunity kept me at home. Not being able to do much in the kitchen or my yard - as a type A personality - was difficult.

Over the years after my treatment, the side effects went away completely except for a small amount of neuropathy in my feet. My husband, daughter, and parents were always there with me, helping and encouraging me. My friends brought lunches from my favorite restaurants. My church family brought us meals. My faith and prayers gave me hope that I would come out on the other side well and whole.

I did not associate with anyone or anything negative. When asked to be on the board of Ovarcome, I felt honored and inspired to be able to tell my story of survival and help other women in their ovarian cancer journey. Ovarcome aligned with my belief in raising awareness and research funds. Volunteering in the GYN clinic once a week and speaking with new patients and their caregivers gave me a sense of helping other women diagnosed with ovarian cancer and sharing hope.

My life perspectives on material gains faded into the background. My family and my faith continued to be most important in my life. It became important for me to let as many people as possible know about the importance of consulting a doctor promptly if you feel something could be wrong with your health. Encouraging others to schedule all annual screenings remains a first and foremost priority.

Ovarcome has given me opportunities to speak out publicly about the importance of awareness and raising research funds for ovarian cancer, sharing the B.E.A.C.H. symptoms, and giving hope to other survivors of ovarian cancer.

My advice to anyone on this journey is to advocate for yourself and your health. Get tested, and seek second opinions. Don't allow negative people to be around you. Think positively about all things in your life. Have courage and hope because research is finding new drugs and drug combinations through clinical trials.

My life perspective is that each day is a gift. Remember that you're not alone on this journey.

I will continue to speak out on behalf of Ovarcome about the importance of raising awareness and research funds to give hope to Ovarcomers. I hope my story will empower other women to listen to their bodies, take charge of their health, and seek medical attention immediately.

> **Try to do the things that you enjoy. It will help you feel normal.**
>
> *- Gloria Salas*

# Gloria Salas

After retaining liquid in her stomach to an unusual amount and increasing difficulty with eating and holding down food, Gloria visited the ER to find a solution. The doctors drained fluids from her stomach and ran several other tests after which Gloria learned the unexpected; she had ovarian cancer.

"I did not expect this. One of the reasons is that I had fallen some time ago and my stomach was inflamed. I went to the hospital and they ran several tests. I was cleared and discharged." she says. Gloria shared that none of her family members are here so she does most of her things by herself.

Following her diagnosis, Gloria began chemotherapy. However, due to several side effects, one of them being her inability to swallow, Gloria returned to taking oral chemo in smaller doses. "The doctors are happy with my progress and say everything is going well so far," she said. She is hopeful for the future, holding faith in her doctors and God.

Despite being alone and being diagnosed with ovarian cancer, Gloria has found ways to keep herself busy and upbeat: "I like to sew and do my little things. I always find something to make me happy. I have my pets and... I try not to think about my diagnosis because it does not help."

She sincerely encourages others in her situation to do the same: "Try to do the things that you enjoy. It will help you feel normal." It was in this upbeat attitude, in this refusal to be beaten by cancer, that Gloria was able to Ovarcome.

When good
things happen,
don't be surprised.
Be satisfied.
Be jubilant.
You deserve it.

> I love to talk to whoever I can get to talk to and seek solace in this journey of Ovarcoming.

— *Zorina Ramcharitar*

# Zorina Ramcharitar

Following a colonoscopy, Zorina began experiencing persistent pain on the right side of her stomach. Despite voicing her concerns during routine visits to her gynecologist, who suggested the pain was due to scar tissue from a prior hysterectomy, Zorina's pain persisted.

With the pain lingering, Zorina advocated for herself and eventually secured an appointment with a doctor in a different town. Her husband explained the situation to the doctor and Zorina was soon put through a CAT scan. Not long after, the unsettling news was delivered—Zorina was diagnosed with stage III ovarian cancer.

Despite facing numerous medical challenges, Zorina was blessed with an abundance of support. Her social worker, siblings, daughter, grandkids, and neighbors stepped in to assist with appointments, commutes, and household chores.

Her husband shouldered the greatest responsibility, juggling his work and caregiving responsibilities simultaneously, taking Zorina to her appointments in between work at the office.

Zorina emphasizes the importance of seeking solace in conversations with others who can relate because each of those conversations helped her push through the tides of pain left in the wake of her diagnosis.

Despite her diagnosis, Zorina is blessed with steadfast love and support, and she wishes others the very best on their journey toward Ovarcoming.

**Inhale Courage.
Exhale Fear.
Ovarcome.**

"

We need to do our part as survivors and Ovarcomers and share our stories so we can help save more lives. There is no cure for ovarian cancer yet, but hopefully one day there will be. Until then, spreading awareness about ovarian cancer is so important. It is your gift to others.

*- Una Buck*

# Una Buck

## Finding out

Una Buck was unexpectedly diagnosed with ovarian cancer stage IIIC. Within a year after diagnosis, she underwent a debulking surgery and six rounds of chemotherapy. When her doctor recommended surgery, he was not 100% sure whether her two tumors were cancerous. "There was just a 50/50 possibility but my oncologist said the tumors had to be removed regardless."

Una's symptoms included frequent urination and feeling uncomfortable anytime she lay on her stomach. "I just assumed I was bloated and had UTI. I did not have a PET scan or biopsy. The tumors were pushing on my bladder which made me urinate so often."

## The journey

When Una went for her yearly check-up, she was tested for UTI and the results showed no infection. "My gynecologist sent me to an urologist and I waited six weeks for an appointment. I wish my doctor would have done an ultrasound earlier, knowing my symptoms. Had she done more to diagnose my symptoms,

I might have been in stage 1 at the time. I've learned that we must work hard and raise our voices to be heard. Looking back I wish I knew more so I could've demanded an ultrasound. But I am forever grateful to the urologist who ordered an ultrasound and then a CT scan. She saved my life."

## Ovarcoming

Una said no matter how smooth-sailing a cancer diagnosis and healing, it's hard. The journey is packed with low and lonely days. "But we are stronger than we know and somehow make it through the hard days, especially when family and friends who love you show up." Una believes in the empowering energy of surrounding oneself with the right people, "your people," she says.

"Don't be afraid to lean on for support, help, and love. Ask it." Since there is no screening for ovarian cancer, most women are not aware of the BEACH symptoms.

## BEACH Symptoms of Ovarian Cancer (created by Ovarcome):

**B** = Bloating

**E** = Early satiety or feeling full quickly

**A** = Abdominal &/or Pelvic Pain

**C** = Changes in Bowel or Bladder Habits

**H** = Heightened fatigue

**Una shares her inspiring message with our community:**

"We need to do our part as survivors and Ovarcomers and share our stories so we can help save more lives. There is no cure for ovarian cancer yet, but hopefully one day there will be. Until then, spreading awareness about ovarian cancer is so important as a survivor. It's your gift to everyone who is still fighting."

"

**Be strong and courageous... pray and ask God for healing... encourage yourself... and do what makes you happy.**

*- Hilda Kangwa*

# Hilda Kangwa

For two months, Hilda felt her stomach bloating. Nothing more and nothing less. But vigilant nonetheless, she asked her sister to take her to the ER. There, she was referred to a gynecologic oncologist and when she visited him, they removed eight bottles of fluid and another nine two weeks later some more.

Finally, after having a total of thirty vials of fluid removed and tested, Hilda's doctors were able to conclude that she had ovarian cancer. "No one has cancer in my family… it was all of a sudden. I was very healthy. Where did this come from?" asks Hilda, confused. Going back and forth between multiple doctors at different hospitals, amidst the noise and confusion, Hilda was finally treated, receiving chemo several times, and undergoing surgery.

However, Hilda was blessed to not have gone through the journey alone. "I have my sister and some friends who come to see me often," says Hilda, "and my sister is there all the time." Having friends and family around, Hilda found solace.

She also found comfort in finding ways to enjoy the simple things of life: solving puzzles, reading stories, and walking outside were a few favorite pastimes of Hilda's that helped her through her journey.

Hilda encourages others like her "To be strong and courageous, to pray for healing and to do what makes you happy." Acknowledging her story as part of a broader collective, Hilda moves forward with a positive outlook, Ovarcoming each obstacle that dares stand in her way.

When I say "I am not ok", don't say "It will be ok" Say, "I am right here until it is"

"

Women don't get checked out enough. I encourage people to go to the doctor and take their health seriously. And stay strong. I look for positive stories like someone who is 10 years healthy. It gives me hope that it could be me.

*- Brittany Hayes*

# Brittany Hayes

## Finding Out

Brittany Hayes faced the unexpected diagnosis of ovarian cancer when she noticed that her stomach seemed very obviously 'lopsided'. She took herself to the ER and her initial assessment revealed an enlarged ovary. A month later, Brittany returned to the ER, this time with a stomach filled with fluid and noticeable swelling. She recalls stomach and bowel issues - that, at first, seemed harmless.

## Journey

From the onset of symptoms to the diagnosis, Brittany's journey spanned only a couple of months. "It's been a struggle, especially when I was in the hospital for a while. I couldn't see my kids because of covid. I couldn't have visitors, so it was just a depressing time. I was on chemo and my immunity took a big hit. I got sick a lot. It was a difficult time."

## Ovarcoming

Despite the challenges of her journey, Brittany maintains hope by focusing on the positive stories of survivors and Ovarcomers. "Women don't get checked out enough. I encourage people to go to the doctor and take their health seriously. And stay strong. I look for positive stories like someone who has been Ovarcoming for 10 years or more. It gives me hope that it could be me."

In navigating her health challenges, Brittany leans on a strong support system from family and friends as she Ovarcomes. "I have people who help me physically and emotionally," she affirmed. As Brittany continues overcoming ovarian cancer, her story stands as a testament to resilience, positivity, and the importance of proactive healthcare.

**What you don't follow Leaves you Behind.**

"

**Be mindful of the symptoms, watch your body, get regular check-ups, and pay it forward by spreading awareness on ovarian cancer.**

*- Angelique Uy*

# Angelique Uy

Due to consistent and severe abdominal pain and having lost a lot of weight, Angelique visited the ER. "I was constipated and there was intense pain in my abdomen which went all the way into my back." After a blood draw, her doctor dismissed her symptoms as a reflux but she was nonetheless sent to the county hospital. After completing a few tests, the doctors determined Angelique had ovarian cancer.

During her first surgery, Angelique bled profusely. Her doctors were unable to complete the procedure and had to close her up for the time being. She was put on chemotherapy. Next year, she was taken in for a hysterectomy. Throughout her cancer journey, Angelique struggled to find sufficient support: "I don't have family here. They are all back in the Philippines and I'm divorced. Sometimes, it is very frustrating, especially to be alone and go through chemo, but I just learned to pray to find strength."

Angelique's mom and brothers tried to provide as much support as they could being far away. But her neighbors, church family, friends, and caregivers filled their roles as much as they could, helping Angelique throughout her journey. She also kept herself busy going on walks, listening to music, and planting in her garden to avoid feeling stressed out.

"It was the pandemic. It was harder to find support then. I'm glad the worst is behind me." Angelique finds hope in clinical trials, thinking they have the potential to serve as "another chance" for her.

Her advice to all women on the same journey is to "be mindful of the symptoms… watch your body… get regular checkups… and pay it forward by spreading awareness on ovarian cancer."

**Say it back:**
**I am strong.**
**I am worthy.**
**I am loved.**
**I am inspiring.**
**I am hopeful.**
**I am proud.**
**I am kind.**
**I am a believer.**
**I am an Ovarcomer!**

"

**Even though you've been diagnosed with cancer, take care of yourself, make it better for yourself.**

*- Christine Kauffman*

# Christine Kauffman

## Finding out

Christine Kauffman's ovarian cancer diagnosis came unexpectedly. She felt something was off when she started losing weight without trying and felt tired all the time. She also had lower abdomen pain that came and went. "Due to the intermittent nature of the pain, I initially thought it was appendicitis."

## Journey

Christine received her diagnosis three months after her first visit to the hospital. Once the diagnosis was made, she was taken in for surgery and a tumor, the size of a two-pound package of hamburger, was removed. Along with it, her appendix and parts of her small and large intestines were also removed.

Reflecting on the signs and symptoms of weight loss and tiredness, Christine thought it was due to her hectic work schedule as she held down two jobs. "I was very busy working two jobs. The weight loss was unexpected, but I initially thought it was due to my workload."

## Ovarcoming

Despite the unfamiliarity of the challenging situation, Christine expressed gratitude for her family and close friends who continued to provide emotional support during her diagnosis and treatment. "I won't say it's easy. But having support in the form of friends and family can make a huge difference to your journey."

Her advice to women on the same path is clear: "Even though you've been diagnosed with cancer, take care of yourself, make it better for yourself." Christine's story is marked by resilience and highlights that no matter what challenges life throws, it's essential to keep Ovarcoming and not give up.

**Do the best you can today.
That is enough.**

> **Stay strong, don't give up.**

— *Anita Reid*

# Anita Reid

While helping a friend move, Anita thought she had pulled a muscle or two causing her to double over in excruciating pain. As the pain persisted, Anita decided to get it checked out. After scans at the hospital, she was diagnosed with ovarian cancer.

Anita had been experiencing symptoms for two months, and although her grandpa had colon cancer and her sister had breast cancer, she says her cancer was not caused by hereditary factors.

During treatment, Anita was diagnosed with carpal tunnel syndrome and had to do extended chemo due to the complications and extreme neuropathy. Even though the diagnosis and treatment were difficult, Anita was blessed with overwhelming support from family and friends, who accompanied her to appointments, helped with chores around the house, and gave her the confidence to keep moving on.

"Stay strong, don't give up," says Anita, and it is with this simple yet powerful and indomitable spirit, that Anita Ovarcomes.

"

Trust your instincts. If you have any inkling that something is wrong, don't talk yourself out of it. I know as women we have a lot of responsibilities. I'm not a mom but my sisters are and I know how busy life can be. But in between your responsibilities towards others, don't forget that you have a responsibility towards yourself as well.

— Yolanda Flyod

# Yolanda Flyod

## Finding Out

Yolanda Floyd's story is a testament to the importance of heeding what your body is trying to tell you and learning to listen to its whispers, no matter how faint. "After a year of job searching, I finally passed the written test and got an offer," she begins. As a final step, she was requested to do a physical exam. Little did she know, this would be the moment that would change everything.

The doctor doing the physical checkup identified something concerning. "I think you have a very large fibroid," he remarked, revealing a potential health hurdle that had gone unnoticed. Recalling her history with fibroids, Yolanda acknowledged that she's had a few large ones in the past as well. The doctor also urged her to investigate further.

## Journey

A chaotic period followed when a physician checked Yolanda and sent her for labs but never contacted her again. During this time, things escalated quickly. She noticed swelling and bloating and was in excruciating pain. All the signs and symptoms became obvious within just two months. "The doctor tried to give me an appointment for mid-December. But when I got home after getting discharged, I had to rush back to emergency a few hours later due to the unbelievable pain."

## Ovarcoming

"I went under the knife right after Thanksgiving.". The healing process, coupled with chemotherapy, brought its own set of challenges, prolonging the road to recovery.

It was a time when Yolanda was struggling with her finances but was grateful for that first physical that kickstarted her investigation into her health.

Reflecting on the onset of symptoms, Yolanda underscores the importance of self-awareness. She initially attributed her aches and pains to age and took a little too long to understand the gravity of the situation.

To those treading a similar path, Yolanda offers heartfelt advice: "Trust your instincts. If you have any inkling that something is wrong, don't talk yourself out of it.

I know as women we have a lot of responsibilities. I'm not a mom but my sisters are and I know how busy life can be. But in between your responsibilities towards others, don't forget that you have a responsibility towards yourself as well. Keep an eye out on your sleep patterns and unusual physical changes – all of them warrant attention."

Yolanda also encourages open conversations among women so they can share experiences and seek support. Yolanda said one of her friends helped her learn how to breathe properly.

Breathing deeply calmed her down and overall helped her be in a better place mentally. "I would encourage people to go online and look for breathing techniques, yoga, and how to develop a positive mindset.

These things help greatly along with the support of family and friends." Yolanda's story is one of resilience, learning, and courage, and confirms, yet again, the power of the right support.

"The support of my sisters and friends has been crucial in going to appointments and getting things done around the house, especially because my post-surgery healing slowed me due to prior chemotherapy. I'm very lucky and grateful for the support system that I have."

I am we.
We are Me.
We Ovarcome
Together.

"

**Live your life day by day and minute by minute. Accept the help you are given and love yourself as much as you can.**

*- Brenda Realyvasquez*

# Brenda Realyvasquez

For Brenda, her ovarian cancer was discovered when she was bloated and "looked nine months pregnant, constipated, and felt uncomfortable in her stomach." She went to her primary care doctor who recommended a CAT scan. "He felt around and didn't like what he was feeling."

Brenda says her condition was so painful that she could barely walk. Right after the CAT scan, the doctor's suspicions were confirmed and Brenda was given the shocking news; she had advanced ovarian cancer.

Brenda said she was lucky to have strong support: "I have my two daughters, one lives with me and helps me a lot and keeps me upbeat, and the other takes me to all my appointments."

Brenda also has two brothers who live with her and provide her with their constant company. She is also surrounded by the support and camaraderie of her church community.

Despite the challenges of being diagnosed with cancer, Brenda was able to power through and Ovarcome, with the love and support of those around her.

To all women and everyone diagnosed with ovarian cancer and walking the same path of Ovarcoming, Brenda's advice is; "Live your life day by day and minute by minute. Accept the help you are given and love yourself as much as you can."

I am more than
a Survivor.
I am an Ovarcomer!

"

The journey is not easy.
Never is. But with the
right support by your
side, you can make
it. Hope should be a
constant companion
if you want to win
and Ovarcome.

*- Crystal Robinson*

# Crystal Robinson

## Finding out

Crystal Robinson woke up to intense stomach pain and bloating. That day marked a full year of discomfort, sleeplessness, and unplanned weight loss. She finally went to the emergency room where her doctor confirmed the inconceivable; she had ovarian cancer. "By this time, the cancer was fully wrapped around my ovaries and uterus. The doctor said it was stage III."

Crystal stayed in pain for a year before getting her first checkup. She assumed it was nothing but constipation and bloating. She kept using over-the-counter medications to "clean herself up" for a long time before realizing it wasn't working and that she needed expert help.

## The Journey

Not knowing how the journey was to unfold, Crystal did not see a doctor immediately after she started noticing the symptoms. This is even though her mother had both breast and lung cancer and passed away at the age of 73. But after diagnosis, she became more proactive about her health and genetic testing. She said, "I'm currently undergoing genetic testing to determine if hereditary factors played a role. The results are still pending."

Opening up about her emotional struggles, Crystal acknowledges the need for counseling after she discovered her health condition and lost her son. "I did not get a chance to mourn him between my surgeries and procedures. Now it's all coming back to me."

## Ovarcoming

Crystal expressed her gratitude for the relentless support of her two daughters and how they remained her steadfast companions throughout the journey. "The girls took care of my medications and my daily chores when I wasn't able to." Her only advice to everyone facing similar challenges was to "never ignore the symptoms" no matter how seemingly minor they may seem.

Crystal's story is about never giving up and always holding onto hope. When one is faced with adversity, one always emerges stronger. "The journey is not easy. Never is. But with the right support by your side, you can make it. Hope should be a constant companion if you want to win this battle against cancer."

> Cancer is not going to beat me. I am not ready to give up.

*- Carol bradshaw*

# Carol bradshaw

Upon her diagnosis, Carol's neighbor took the role of her primary caregiver, going above and beyond as they navigated this unforeseen journey together. And meanwhile, her son, daughter-in-law, and grandchild, living nearby, provided Carol with their loving support. Daily communication with her sister added another layer of connection to her support system.

"I talk up a storm with my sister every day," Carol says, emphasizing her appreciation for her close connection with her sister. Confronting a stage three ovarian cancer diagnosis at the age of sixty-nine, Carol opted for a path illuminated by hope. Her positive attitude emerged as her guiding light on the journey to Ovarcoming. While cancer may have quietly infiltrated her life, she, in turn, declared her resolution not to be conquered.

She wants to be around for her son. She wants to be around for her sister. She wants to see her grandson grow up to be the fine man she knows he will grow up to be. "Cancer is not going to beat me," she says, "I am not ready to give up."

The vision propelling Carol forward is clear, and it is with this vision that she ovarcomes. With hope firmly in her grasp, Carol soon turned toward clinical trials. Carol found the clinical trials to offer a glimmer of hope amidst her life-changing diagnosis.

Carol encourages others to consider clinical trials as well, urging others to seize any opportunity to help themselves out of the horrible mess of diagnosis.

"Have a positive attitude, you are going to Ovarcome."

You can't repair.
You can't restore.
You can't rebuild.
If you don't b-r-e-a-k.

> Don't dismiss your symptoms. Don't assume you know what's causing the issue. I now wish I had been more aggressive with my health.

*- Deborah Merrill*

# Deborah Merrill

## Finding Out

Deborah Merrill's ovarian cancer was diagnosed accidentally. She found herself in the ER with acute pain in her lower right abdomen which she initially thought was caused by diverticulitis. An ultrasound revealed a fibroid on her uterus. "I have gastroparesis and so I thought this may be caused by my condition. So I made an appointment with my gastrologist. He said he did not want to do a colonoscopy because I had had one a year ago. He said if I had cancer, it would have been detected at that time."

## Journey

Deborah was recommended to see her gynecologist who conducted a thorough checkup and sent her scans to an oncologist. The news came back that Deborah had cancer. Apart from lower abdomen pain, Deborah also had pain in her lower back when she sat down. "I've had hemorrhoids for a long time and when I wasn't careful when sitting down, I felt a sharp pain.

I kept ignoring my back pain for at least a year. I should've seen a doctor sooner." From her first visit to the hospital for abdomen pain, it took Deborah one month to be diagnosed.

## Ovarcoming

Deborah said, "I've only been alone about four days after I visited the hospital. But my daughter is always with me. And if she isn't, then my granddaughter or my significant other are. They help do the housework. A few days after chemo, I'm not in the best shape so they take care of me during that time."

When asked what advice she would share with our community of women going through what she has to help and encourage them, Deborah said, "Don't dismiss your symptoms. Don't assume you know what's causing the issue. I now know I should have been more aggressive for my health."

Love is the virtue
of the heart.
Ovarcoming is the
virtue of the spirit.

"
**Go get checked.**

*- Carolyn Selman*

# Carolyn Selman

Unsure of what was going on with her body, Carolyn, after experiencing symptoms for three or four days, decided to take action. "I went to the ER, but they weren't sure so they sent me to the Cancer Center," she says. She had been experiencing stomach swelling and unusual tiredness and wanted to know what was going on. Carolyn experienced a few of the classic B.E.A.C.H. symptoms of ovarian cancer:

**B** = Bloating

**E** = Early Satiety or feeling full quickly

**A** = Abdominal &/or Pelvic Pain

**C** = Changes in Bowel/Bladder Habits

**H** = Heightened Fatigue

After her tests, Carol was given the life changing news. She had ovarian cancer. Having done genetic testing, Carolyn said "it was negative," and determined that the roots of her cancer were not hereditary.

"Go get checked all the time," she advises everyone, stressing the need to be vigilant and on the watch for any sign, no matter how trivial.

Despite her diagnosis, she persevered to keep a positive state of mind. With the strong social support from family and friends, along with the compassion, care, and guidance of a social worker at her hospital, Carolyn was able to walk this difficult path with hope.

It was through her determination and the strength she found in those around her, that Carolyn was able to Ovarcome.

**Count the dreams
of happiness and
keep the doors open
to miracles.**

" I was losing all my hair and trying to hide it with a cap. But my grandson is a smart kid. One day he asked 'Why are you always wearing a hat Gigi?' and I told him Gigi has cancer and that I was going through chemo. It's going to take away my hair, I told him, but I'm still going to be here. So when I finally showed him my head he said 'Oh Gigi, it doesn't look bad at all, you look cute." That made me smile.

*- Carla Staten*

# Carla Staten

## Finding Out

Carla Staten's ovarian cancer journey started when she noticed a few 'knots' on both sides of her hips. She went to the doctor for a diagnosis and was quickly dismissed. She was told that they were just swollen lymph nodes and would go away on their own. But the knots persisted and grew in size.

Three months and a CT scan later, she learned that she had masses on both ovaries. "I was grateful that I had no further symptoms beyond the knots. There was no pain and I thank God for this every day."

## Journey

From the initial discovery of symptoms in December to ovarian cancer diagnosis in March, Carla's journey of Ovarcoming was swift and marked by faith and hope.

Carla continues to draw positivity from the people around her and her story is a testament to the importance of finding inner strength. "I already knew I would lose all my hair after chemo, but it takes time to get used to some changes. It's a transition. Having faith and staying positive is the key to getting to the other side."

Carla said she is very grateful that she did not have any pain throughout her journey. Her doctors thought it was a miracle. This renewed her faith in God. But one of the hardest things, she said, has been missing her grandson's games after chemotherapy started. "I was losing all my hair and trying to hide it with a cap. But my grandson is a smart kid. One day he asked 'Why are you always wearing a hat Gigi?' and I told him Gigi has cancer and that I was going through chemo. It's going to take away my hair, I told him, but I'm still going to be here. So when I finally showed him my head he said 'Oh Gigi, it doesn't look bad at all, you look cute.'" That made me smile.

## Ovarcoming

Carla appreciates the strong social support she receives from her family and through programs that help her with transportation to and from appointments and chemotherapy. Having participated in a clinical trial, Carla believes in the importance of research for the benefit of others.

Her advice to women facing a similar journey is rooted in strength and faith. "My mother was a cancer survivor and Ovarcomer for 17 years. She has been my biggest inspiration for how she believed in God even when things got tough. I've seen her in excruciating pain. But she survived. She did Ovarcome. And because of her, I've learned to stay strong and not give into despair." Carla's story is one of strength and gratitude and highlights how a positive mindset can help improve the quality of life, even when things get tough.

**❝**

**Looking at a nice sunset or sunrise is a blessing in my life. Life's beauty is in its little things.**

*- Chun Chu Ha*

# Chun Chu Ha

After a colonoscopy, Chun Chu's stomach became quite bloated. She thought it was simply a complication of the colonoscopy. But after sensing her doctor's concern, she took a blood test and saw that her calcium levels were abnormally high. With this news, Chun Chu went to the ER to receive a CAT scan. Chun Chu was diagnosed with ovarian cancer.

"I was getting bloated, felt frequently tired, was losing weight, and had to go to the bathroom often," she recalls, tracing back to the symptoms that eventually led to her diagnosis.

These symptoms had been present for several months. "As far as they could tell, it wasn't genetic."

However, despite the challenge and uncertainty of diagnosis, Chun Chu was surrounded with love and support: "My family and friends would take me to appointments, help with household chores, bring me food, and spend time with me quite often.

Chun Chu found beauty in enjoying the simple things of life. She says, "Looking at a nice sunset or sunrise is a blessing in my life."

She puts her trust in her physician even when times get tough, and has found peace in "trusting the process." "I was not the first one and I won't be the last," she says, but she perseveres with a positive mindset, in the hope that someday, all women like her will be cured.

**Hope or Hope Postponed – hope always surrounds us even if it arrives late.**

> Stay positive no matter what. I've found that if I keep a positive mindset the outcome is not as traumatic, I don't get depressed as often, and I don't get sick as often. I know I can survive another day as I continue to Ovarcome. I am not willing to give up.

*- Jacqueline Day*

# Jacqueline Day

## Finding out

Jacqueline Day's ovarian cancer was diagnosed when she had to rush to the ER with severe lower abdomen pains. A CAT scan revealed a tumor slightly larger than a basketball attached to her left ovary. Three weeks later, she was in surgery for a hysterectomy. "The doctors removed the tumor. But the cancer had spread into my small intestines. They started me on six-month chemotherapy and infusion therapy and I was finally declared cancer-free almost a year later. I was scheduled for regular check-ins lest the cancer returned."

## Journey

Two years later, Jacqueline found herself in the ER once again with agonizing lower abdomen pains, vomiting, and constipation. Due to her history of cancer, she was immediately taken for a CAT scan and she was told that a new tumor was found in her small intestines over a strangulated hernia. She was taken in for emergency surgery. "They took out nine inches of small intestines with the hernia.

I got started on infusion therapy again. Six months later, another CAT scan revealed new tumors on the liver, in between the pancreas and the gallbladder, and two more on the small intestines.

The number of tumors had gone from one to five in just a few months. I've given birth to two children. And the pain of childbirth pales in comparison to what I went through at the time."

## Ovarcoming

After the surgery, Jacqueline faced issues like brittle and weak nails that kept breaking off, hair loss, and skin pallor. In the process, she said her urethra was cut by accident and she had a fistula and had to wear a catheter and diapers for six months.

She also got a bladder infection which turned into septic shock. "I've endured it all over the last 6 years. It's unbelievable."

After Jacqueline completed her infusion therapy, she started chemotherapy pills. Her tumors have shrunk by half and the prognosis is good, but the doctors believe she may have to remain on medicine all her life. "The only way forward is to keep it in control for as long as possible through medicines."

Jacqueline shared, "I have a great support system, not family-wise as my parents are deceased and my youngest son is pretty much the only family I have in this area. But my cancer doctor has set me up with support care with other cancer patients and I have friends in my network. They are sympathetic and help with anything that I need help with so I am very blessed."

"Stay positive no matter what. I've found that if I keep a positive mindset the outcome is not as traumatic, I don't get depressed as often, and I don't get sick as often, I keep fighting this because it's a fight for my life and I know I can survive another day if I keep fighting. I've had friends give up and they just went downhill really fast. I'm not willing to do that."

> **Being able to talk to others going through the same thing has really made me feel good.**
>
> *- Crystal Wardrick*

# Crystal Wardrick

Crystal experienced heavy bleeding, excessive urination, and the loss of a significant amount of weight. Upon visiting the doctor, she was told that she was merely experiencing heavy periods. She was promptly dismissed with birth control pills to control her hormones. But one night, as Crystal rolled over her stomach in bed, she felt a large lump on the side of her stomach.

"It felt like a baseball on the right side of my stomach," Crystal recalls. She visited the doctor once more and received an ultrasound. Upon reviewing the results, her doctor said that they "needed to get her tested as soon as possible.

Once the tests were completed, the doctor delivered the news: Crystal had ovarian cancer. After a hysterectomy and six months of chemo, Crystal's doctor, after examination, discovered two spots on her liver, which soon grew to an undeniable size.

After a liver biopsy, Crystal's doctors determined the cancer had metastasized to her liver as well as into her diaphragm. The tumors were promptly removed, and Crystal, having part of her diaphragm removed, began to have difficulty breathing. But after two weeks on a ventilator, her condition began to improve.

"I was telling them what was going on for a whole year," says Crystal, emphasizing the necessity to get diagnosed as early as possible. But more than this, Crystal says "Prayer, eating better, drinking plenty of water, and finding support groups can be lifesavers." They helped her power through her journey.

"Being able to talk to other ladies going through the same thing has really made me feel good," says Crystal. It's for her son that she continues to "fight and hold on to life" and keeps the hope alive to Ovarcome.

**Make hope stronger than your coffee.**

“

We all have trials and tribulations that happen in our lives. But how we respond to them is everything. Maintaining a positive attitude and expecting the best rather than the worst really helps.

*- Joanna Casalini*

# Joanna Casalini

## Finding Out

Joanna Casalini's pregnancy with her son took an unexpected turn during one of her regular ultrasounds. She was 26 weeks pregnant when the radiologist found an unusual mass in one of her ovaries. She referred Joanna to a specialist. Joanna said she had no signs or symptoms whatsoever, and according to her, the cancer's presentation mirrored pregnancy symptoms, making it impossible to tell if anything was wrong.

Further diagnosis was halted for the time being due to her pregnancy and the doctors recommended waiting until her son reached gestational age safe for further procedures. "At 36 weeks, doctors took me for a C-section, and the mass was also removed. During the 10 weeks when it was first spotted and then finally removed, it had grown quickly and was massive. It was three times the size of my newborn son."

## Journey

Joanna said her husband and their extended family, who live locally, have been very supportive throughout her journey. "My husband provided crucial assistance during this entire period along with both our families. The help and support carried us through at the time with a newborn and the challenges of cancer treatment."

## Ovarcoming

During that time, the family mostly stayed in, receiving meals and support from loving family members and friends. Psycho-social counseling, a vital service, is already part of Joanna's support system and helps her cope considerably with her ongoing treatments.

Joanna's advice for others facing similar challenges is this: "We all have trials and tribulations that happen in our lives. But how we respond to them is everything. Maintaining a positive attitude and expecting the best rather than the worst really helps." This wisdom encapsulates her resilient approach to navigating the challenges of her cancer journey.

The spirit of Ovarcoming is like a warm blanket on a cold night.

"Keep your faith and know that even if there are bad days, you will ovarcome it - even when you feel like you are not going to.

— *Daijha Marshall*

# Daijha Marshall

After moving to another city, Daijha began to experience pain in her lower abdomen. "My abdominal pain was excruciating. I couldn't sleep, I couldn't get out of bed, or bend over," says Daijha, and her pain soon drove her to the hospital.

There, the doctors told her she had a mass on her ovaries and scheduled her for emergency surgery to have it removed. All of this happened over two weeks. Once her pathology report came back two weeks later, the doctors told her that her cancer was malignant. "It was a germ cell tumor and because it had ruptured, it had become cancerous," Daijha added.

The doctors directed her to chemotherapy. Although she has no family history, Daijha was able to catch her symptoms early and was diagnosed within two weeks of sensing the symptoms. Her friends and family provided her with all the support they could offer, keeping her company and driving her to her appointments.

"Keep your faith and know that even if there are bad days, you will ovarcome them," says Daijha, "you'll beat it even when you feel like you are not going to." It is with this unwavering faith that Daijha perseveres, and it is through this positivity that she Ovarcomes.

Face the storm.
Hold your head high.
Summon the
courage to continue.
Embrace the
indomitable spirit of
Ovarcoming.

"
Listen to your body. Listen to what it's telling you and then do what you need to do. And just don't give up and you will get through it.

— Barbara Hauser

# Barbara Hauser

## Finding Out

Barbara Hauser's diagnosis came unexpectedly when she sought medical attention for shortness of breath, leading to the discovery of fluid in her lungs. Subsequent hospital visits revealed cancer cells in the lung fluid and stage IV cancer. Despite the initial shock, Barbara braved the treatment, managing to undergo multiple hospital stays and rounds of chemotherapy.

"They removed almost two liters of fluid during my first visit for shortness of breath and sent me on my way. Four days later, I was back in the Emergency with the same issue. They removed the fluid again and gave me the devastating news."

Barbara was having frequent spasms on the right side of her body along with continued shortness of breath for months. She knew that something was not right even though her doctors dismissed her symptoms as nothing serious. Her persistence led to her eventual diagnosis.

## Journey

In Barbara's case, cancer had spread from her ovaries into her lungs. "My primary care doctor said it's very difficult to detect ovarian cancer in its initial stages." Upon diagnosis, her doctor advised immediate chemotherapy.

Luckily for Barbara, the results have been promising. "We kept doing regular CAT scans to see if all was well and the doctor said the cancer is shrinking." But despite the success, the side effects of chemo were "brutal" for her. The reality of treatment may be harsh, but keeping hope on her side, Barbara kept on Ovarcoming.

## Ovarcoming

In the face of adversity, Barbara's advice to all diagnosed is clear: "Never ignore the symptoms, no matter how seemingly minor they may seem." She stresses the need for early detection, underscoring her own experience of delayed diagnosis. Despite the side effects of the treatment, she understood the importance of fighting through, echoing the encouragement she received from her medical team and loved ones.

As Barbara continues to Ovarcome ovarian cancer, her story inspires hope and is a reminder to anyone (not just those with ovarian cancer) that with courage and support, one can navigate and Ovarcome just about anything.

> **Find a good support system. It will get you through to the other side.**

*- Denise Evans*

# Denise Evans

Denise's story began when she started experiencing shortness of breath and visited her pulmonologist. Her doctor ordered a thoracentesis, where fluid was collected for culture. After the fluid was tested, the doctors came back to Denise and delivered the news: she had ovarian cancer.

But despite the weight of the news, Denise was diagnosed in less than a month after she began to have difficulty breathing. Having done genetic testing, Denise found out her cancer was not hereditary. It was a challenging phase but Denise had a strong circle of social support to help her push through.

She sees hope in clinical trials: "I think they are a great thing because finding new meds that might help someone with ovarian cancer… it's a good thing."

Denise encourages others on the journey to be vigilant. "If you feel lower back pain… get an ultrasound done and find a good support system. It will get you through to the other side."

> Just don't give up.
> Do a lot of praying and
> have faith. Hold on.

— *Katherine Anaya*

# Katherine Anaya

## Finding Out

Katherine Anaya's ovarian cancer diagnosis took a long time. It all began when she sought help for sharp pains in her back, nausea, and persistent vomiting. This was her third visit to the emergency room. On this day, she was finally referred to a Specialist. Her doctor initially suspected that there was an issue with her gallbladder.

## Journey

Further investigations revealed something more serious. Katherine recalls, "The doctor said we may have to remove the gallbladder altogether. But when she started the exploratory surgery she did not remove the gallbladder. She just took some biopsy samples. Soon after, she asked me to go to an Oncologist, which I did."

## Ovarcoming

Despite her visibly frailing health, it took Katherine a full year before she was diagnosed with ovarian cancer. For her, genetic testing became even more essential because her mother passed away due to ovarian cancer as well. Katherine shared she has the loving support of her family as she Ovarcomes, "My daughter here, she's the main one. I'm grateful for her support."

When asked what her number one advice is to women trying to Ovarcome just like her, she said, "Just don't give up. Keep praying and holding on. Have faith."

Let go of your plan.
Embrace change.
If it doesn't open, it
is not your door -
don't knock.
Do more of what
you love.

> Accept your illness and what you are going to go through with treatments. Take your doctor's advice. Don't listen to people discouraging or underestimating what you are going through.

*- Eman Khatab*

# Eman Khatab

Eman began to notice unusual discharges, instances of bleeding, sharp pains in her lower abdomen, and pain in her back and legs. She promptly went to the hospital with her husband.

But both her husband and her doctor dismissed her symptoms as nothing to be concerned about. Eman was handed a few antibiotics to help resolve the issue.

But while on a trip to Egypt, Eman's symptoms began to worsen. Eman visited a family doctor in Egypt, who, after tests and imaging, concluded Eman had ovarian cancer. Although he offered to treat Eman in Egypt, she knew she would soon be leaving for the US in the next month. After returning to her doctor in the US, and after repeating the same set of tests, Eman's US doctor concluded the same; she had ovarian cancer.

Thereafter, Eman was advised of surgery and started chemotherapy. In the US, Eman had no family or friends. There were moments when her diagnosis was downplayed, or when she received negative comments that hurt her feelings.

But despite the lack of support and understanding, Eman fought through her pain by finding strength in herself. "Accept your illness and what you are going to go through with treatments. Take your doctor's advice. Don't listen to people discouraging or underestimating what you are going through. Believe in the higher powers to guide you in this path of Ovarcoming."

**Keep Living.**
**Keep Hoping.**
**Keep Asking.**
**Keep Believing.**
**Keep Inspiring.**

> Mandi Chambless, with the indomitable spirit of Ovarcoming, summited Everest Base Camp in 2023 inspiring many along the journey.

*- Mandi Chambless*

# Mandi Chambless

"You are too young and you have no family history."

"This may just be the way you are now."

"It's probably just a temporary gastrointestinal issue."

These are just a few of the assumptions that were made by the multiple doctors that misdiagnosed me. Unfortunately, these assumptions led to a near-fatal turn of events for me. These assumptions were made over three months as my ovaries raged against themselves and the rest of my body.

These assumptions nearly killed me.

For three months I continued to push for answers, even when it seemed as if I would never get any.

My lower back was aching, my stomach was getting bigger, I felt like I could pee on command, and I was excessively fatigued. Through it all, I remained my own advocate. After all, if we aren't our own advocates, who will be?

An ultrasound was finally scheduled and a mass was finally found. Even then, "Don't worry, you are too young and you have no family history. It's not cancer."

Surgery was recommended and scheduled but even as I was put under, I had no clue what I'd wake up to. When the haze of anesthesia lifted for a split second in the recovery room, I overheard, "28-year-old female, malignant neoplastic ovaries," the nurse next to my bed stated. Oh no, she's talking about me…I thought as the anesthesia took hold again. That's how I found out I had cancer.

Stage IIIc high-grade serous carcinoma. A very aggressive form of ovarian cancer - called the silent killer. Because I was young, the diagnosis was dismissed for three months as the cancer metastasized to my omentum, bowels, and lymph nodes. The truth is, I am beyond lucky to still be alive because the stats are grim, indicating that I had about a 20% chance of living 5 years.

Friends, that was more than a decade and a half ago. My expiration date may have been stamped on the minds of my doctors, but life had other plans for me. I had six rounds of intraperitoneal chemo that was chock full of unpleasant side effects, I have struggled with emotional wounds that have left behind obvious scars.

But I am still alive.

I am still alive, even as I have borne witness to those around me who suffer and pass away from this very disease. I've held the hands of those undergoing chemo and I've had numerous patients and caregivers reach out to me for guidance and support on social media. I've drained the fluid buildup caused by ovarian cancer from my best friend's abdomen and I've also spoken on stage at her celebration of life after she passed away.

Yet I am still here.

People have asked me what it's like to be an Ovarcomer. I think it's different for all of us. We don't escape our journeys unscathed, of course. We have been poked and prodded, we have been gutted like fish. Our bodies are battered and bruised and unrecognizable to us. We are traumatized. We live in fear of recurrence. No, we don't get off the cancer ride to return to what we were before but we also live in hope, praying that one day that cure will come. Praying that one day we will stop having to watch those that we love pass away from this relentless disease.

It is insufficient to simply call us cancer survivors. We survive so much more than the cancer itself. I survived learning what my new normal is, even as I still work to figure out what that means. I survived a divorce shortly after I finished chemo because my ex-husband wasn't strong enough to honor me "in sickness and in health." I survived picking up, moving to a new city by myself, and starting my life over, literally from scratch.

Surviving means traveling, paying it forward, setting an example. It's accepting my past, allowing it to mold me, and guiding me to become better than what I probably would have been without it. Surviving means not taking anything for granted.

Over a decade. A blink of an eye. To most people, it doesn't sound that long but to us and the people who love us, it is a lifetime. I will honor and respect with grace the time I have been given. I won't waste a second of it and I will do it for them. I will not take this opportunity that others aren't always fortunate enough to be gifted lightly.

"I want to inspire people. I want someone to say, "Because of you, I didn't give up."

> **Whether for a few months or a few years, we are here to Ovarcome.**

— *Penelope gomez*

# Penelope gomez

Having already been diagnosed with kidney cancer, the thought of ovarian cancer did not arise in her mind. "I just had a little abdominal pain each time I exercised, but the pain was persistent and would not go away" After a physical exam, and several tests, Penelope was diagnosed with ovarian cancer - her symptoms were subtle.

Penelope's grandmother passed away from stomach cancer, her mother from ovarian cancer, and her aunt from colon cancer. With a strong family history, Penelope tested positive for the BRCA1 mutation.

During this journey of diagnosis and treatment, Penelope's sister, husband, and neighbor provided their unwavering support, taking her to medical appointments, helping with household chores, and surrounding her with their love and friendship. Despite the adversity, Penelope kept a positive mindset and pushed through. "Try to experience positive things," Penelope says, "Whether, for a few months or a few years, we are all here to Ovarcome."

Penelope chooses to be an Ovarcomer. She follows her doctor's recommendations, gets plenty of rest, keeps her every medical appointment, and makes it a point to eat healthy.

Penelope resolves to do everything that is in her power to control. With the loving support of her family and friends, Penelope faces every challenge with the motivation to Ovarcome.

Sow the seed of hope. It may not bear fruit today. But it will surely lead you to the path to Ovarcome.

"

Take all the help that you can get. It's a lot to go through. Cancer changes you in many ways.
I went from being very active and social, working full-time 50 hours a week, exercising thrice weekly, and being a grandma and a caregiver to my mom, to being sick. I've never really been sick before and it was a lot to adjust to. It takes a lot out of you, not only your physical vibrance but it puts you in a different place mentally.

*- Cheri Ferris*

# Cheri Ferris

Cheri Ferris's ovarian cancer was discovered unexpectedly and by accident. "I got sick one weekend after moving heavy furniture," she recounts. "I thought I had pulled a muscle as I had excruciating pain on my right side and I was throwing up due to the pain. I went to the ER, and they found a tumor that was larger than a grapefruit attached to my fallopian tubes, uterus, and the outside of my colon."

Reflecting on her symptoms, Cheri notes a prolonged period of fatigue that she initially attributed to her demanding lifestyle as she cared for her mother in hospice while working full-time and being a grandmother. "I had been tired for a long time, for months, like fatigued.

I kept falling asleep at my desk," she shares. Cheri now realizes it was probably a sign of something more serious than just being overworked. Cheri shares that on her visits to her gynecologist, she was told that she was menopausal and her periods were going to be irregular, so she was mentally prepared for changes to come.

The path to diagnosis took approximately seven months. She says balancing work, health, and the adjustments to working from home have proven challenging, but Cheri tackles each day with resilience.

Cheri acknowledges the vital role of clinical trials in advancing cancer treatments, given her personal experience with chemotherapy reactions. "All of my medications I'm on have gone through clinical trials," she states. While she hasn't considered enrolling in trials yet, she acknowledges their significance in refining treatment options.

Amidst her journey of Ovarcoming, Cheri found strength in the support of her family and friends.

"I do have strong social support," she affirms, highlighting the importance of accepting help and seeking counseling to cope with the profound changes cancer brings.

In closing, Cheri offers advice to those on a similar journey, "Take all the help that you can get. It's a lot to go through. Cancer changes you in many ways. I went from being very active and social, working full-time 50 hours a week, exercising thrice weekly, and being a grandma and a caregiver to my mom, to being sick.

I've never really been sick before and it was a lot to adjust to. It takes a lot out of you, not only your physical vibrance but it puts you in a different place mentally." Cheri's story is one of hope and not giving up. Her story proves, yet again, that the human spirit can be resilient and triumphant even in the face of daunting challenges.

> **If you feel something is wrong with your body, get to it sooner.**
>
> *- Lisa Behrens*

# Lisa Behrens

Lisa Behrens received her ovarian cancer diagnosis after experiencing swelling in her left leg and her lower pelvic area. Lisa decided to visit her doctor to figure out what was causing it. Her doctor recommended she take a few tests but the results were inconclusive. She sent Lisa to an ob-gyn who did a pap smear and a biopsy of her uterus but found nothing. Certain there was something wrong, Lisa then visited the general surgeon of her town who did a needle biopsy of her pelvic region. That's when Lisa first heard the word 'cancer'.

Although the doctors were uncertain about the type of cancer and kept "flipping back and forth from peritoneal to ovarian" cancer, they officially confirmed that Lisa had ovarian cancer during a hysterectomy - a procedure Lisa had previously requested due to the development of ovarian cysts and the excruciating cramps that followed.

Years ago when she had gone to her doctor for cyclic cramps, she was prescribed medication to alleviate the pain but it turned out that the source of her problem was something else entirely. "At the time my cysts had enlarged and I'm fairly positive that they were bursting. Issues were going on inside me that took quite a while to be diagnosed completely."

Despite the challenges, Lisa has hope in clinical trials "clinical trials are going to be one of my best chances." Lisa with help of several counselors, family, and friends, has persevered despite the odds.

To every person on the same journey as her, Lisa advises not to take no for an answer. "If you feel something is wrong with your body, listen to your gut, and get to it sooner."

Life is Good.
Cancer, you don't
have power.
I don't just fight
you and Survive.
I Ovarcome.

> It is hard to keep your spirits up during your diagnosis and chemo, but having support from family is essential to getting to the other side. My mom keeps my spirits up. When I feel low, I talk to her, and she guides me, saying, 'Don't give up. A lot of times, you need that external validation. You want to hear that you can do it.

*- Nichelle Dragon*

# Nichelle Dragon

## Finding Out

When bloating and persistent coughing troubled Nichelle Dragon, she initially thought it was bronchitis. Her family doctor prescribed antibiotics, but the symptoms did not go away and she "felt like they got worse over a week". Concerned, Nichelle found herself in the emergency room. She underwent a CAT scan which revealed a tumor in her ovaries.

Apart from bloating and coughing, Nichelle said she didn't experience any other symptoms. "I had no idea I'd have ovarian cancer. The diagnosis was unexpected, to say the least." Reflecting on her journey, she shared, "I started noticing symptoms over Christmas and waited too long to see my doctor. I was diagnosed in the first week of January, and my surgery followed on the 15th of the month."

## Journey

Throughout this challenging time, her family and friends remained her pillars of support. "My boyfriend takes me to all my appointments and my mom and dad help out around the house when I need something or when I'm not feeling good. I feel lucky to have a lot of support."

Offering advice to women facing a similar journey, Nichelle emphasized the crucial role of support. "It's hard to keep your spirits up during your diagnosis and chemo, but having support from family is essential to getting to the other side. My mom keeps my spirits up. When I feel low, I talk to her, and she guides me, saying, 'Don't give up; you're going to beat this. A lot of times, you need that external validation. You want to hear that you can do it.'"

## Ovarcoming

"It is important to have someone to talk to and someone to tell you that it will be alright. You will get through it. These simple words can lend you a lot of strength when things get tough."

Nichelle's story once again highlights the significance of a robust support system during the trials and tribulations of ovarian cancer. Her resilience, coupled with the encouragement from her loved ones, serves as an inspiration to others.

"Ask for help. Don't try to do it alone. You don't have to."

> **Stay positive and always be strong.**
>
> *- Houa Thao*

# Houa Thao

In the beginning, Houa did not understand she was seriously sick: "I just went to the hospital and they told me," she says.

Despite the sudden diagnosis, Houa had been experiencing the symptoms for a year: loss of appetite, jaundice, and stomach swelling plagued her. "I was the first person to have this in my family," Houa says. Her cancer was not genetic.

In the midst of many adversities brought about by her diagnosis, Houa's family was supportive and her loving husband took her to each of her appointments. To find strength in her journey, Houa reaches out to women and talks to them, carries out her days just as she used to before the health challenges, and remains optimistic in treatment.

"Stay positive and always be strong," Houa says. It is by this philosophy that Houa was able to push through her journey, as would a true Ovarcomer.

> Take it a day at a time, an hour at a time.

>> *- Crystal Stanley*

# Crystal Stanley

## Finding Out

For Crystal Stanley, the discovery of ovarian cancer was a long and winding road. While the symptoms surfaced, the official diagnosis didn't materialize until many months later. A trip to the ER revealed a mass which led to a series of surgeries. Despite removing the cancer, it persisted. The official confirmation of her diagnosis came after an extensive review process that involved tumor boards and consultations with multiple medical institutions.

## Journey

More than anything else, Crystal's journey with ovarian cancer was marked by unpredictability. It began with sporadic incidents like persistent pain in her lower abdomen and a ruptured cyst. However, the intermittent pain in her lower abdomen intensified, reaching a point where she struggled to walk or function normally.

The persistent pain led her to the emergency room, revealing a substantial mass. Multiple surgeries followed, removing everything, yet the cancer persisted, challenging the conventional understanding of its recurrence post-hysterectomy.

## Ovarcoming

Crystal's advice to women navigating a similar path is simple yet profound: "Take it a day at a time, an hour at a time." This encapsulates the resilience required to confront the uncertainties that accompany a cancer diagnosis. Her uncertainties during cancer diagnosis, recovery, and remission challenged Crystal to go within and find strength. Her advice to anyone facing the unknown is the same; "Take a breather and take it one step at a time." Crystal's story invites reflection on the importance of taking things slow, embracing the support that surrounds you, and remaining open to new possibilities, even amid the unknown.

Took one day
to be told.
"You have cancer".
Takes every day.
To Ovarcome.

> Take care of your mental health in this journey of Ovarcoming.
> You are not alone.

— *Karen Aho*

## Karen Aho

Amid the pandemic, Karen Aho experienced the symptoms of ovarian cancer for nine months before being diagnosed. At first, she thought her discomfort and bloating were just part of getting older, a normal part of perimenopause, but soon, she learned it was something more serious.

This is a story of hope, of resilience, of overcoming silent struggles. This is the story of Karen's journey. "I thought it was just perimenopause," Karen shares, thinking the subtle signs were just a part of aging. But ovarian cancer quietly entered her life, affecting her exercise and causing persistent bloating. The chaos of the pandemic made it hard to catch these signs early, delaying Karen's diagnosis. Living on her own, Karen was forced to face daily challenges with pain and discomfort.

She noted that "Sometimes people say things that make us feel guilty or upset, making us believe we caused our cancer." Thankfully, her friends and her brother's regular visits brought comfort during the tough times, and Karen realized the importance of "staying positive and avoiding stress."

During her journey with ovarian cancer, Karen found comfort not just in her loved ones but also by distancing herself from negativity, embracing a positive mindset, and reducing unnecessary stress. The biggest lesson from Karen's journey is about catching things early: "I lost about a whole year before getting diagnosed with ovarian cancer," she reveals, emphasizing the need for awareness. But despite this delay, and the challenges of the pandemic, Karen emerged victorious, stronger than she'd ever been.

Karen took part in clinical trials for closer monitoring - a proactive measure ensuring more frequent scans and comprehensive evaluations. She encourages others to do the same, to benefit from the careful attention and the strategic approaches she was offered to ensure her a happy and healthy rest of her life.

In this story, Karen isn't just a survivor; she's an Ovarcomer - a testament to the human spirit to face life's challenges with an unwavering attitude of strength and positivity.

Through her words, Karen inspires not only those with ovarian cancer but also anyone in tough times, offering a light of hope in the storm of diagnosis.

> I've learned how sweet the little things in life are. To experience my grandchildren's firsts and spend so much time with them each week. To feel the warmth of the sun on my skin at our favorite RV site in Port Aransas. To wake up to the sweet smell of coffee every day, thanks to my husband of 35 years. Life is sweet, even in the midst of the tough stuff. And that's what I'd like to remember, all the while acknowledging the difficult, painful, and long journey that this continues to be.

*- Debbie Bisbano*

# Debbie Bisbano

## Finding out

You never think that it's going to be you; the one diagnosed with cancer. But there I sat, diagnosed with Stage 4a ovarian cancer and found to have the BRCA1 genetic mutation. Once the dust settled and all of the information sunk in, I decided that I could frame this next part of my life how I wanted, instead of letting it frame me. That's when I knew the journey ahead was just that, my journey.

What started as a debulking surgery and initial rounds of chemotherapy has turned into what seems like an on-again off-again relationship with something I never even wanted in the first place. But, with the support and love of those around me, I've been able to keep moving forward on my journey.

Let me backup and start from the beginning…

# Journey

After several months of misdiagnoses and having to become my advocate, I was finally diagnosed and could start my treatment with my amazing care team. I received 9 rounds of chemotherapy, a debulking surgery then 9 more rounds of chemo to complete my first fight against this beast. My husband and I had nearly just retired and moved into a new home which unfortunately meant long commutes for chemo and doctor appointments but… with my husband by my side, we made it through.

I was aware from the beginning that ovarian cancer is such a beast because of its nature to keep coming back. Despite this, I maintained my faith and positive attitude. And despite this, the beast came back. But again, I put on my fighting pants and made it through. I could tell you all the details, the ugly nitty gritty of what it's like to go through treatment not just once, but five separate times. But instead, I want to share what I've learned during this time; the bright spots I clung to and continue to cling to today.

## Ovarcoming

I've learned that when times are tough, the human spirit is tougher. That my friends really and truly would do anything for me. From sending helpful gifts to getting me through chemotherapy, to taking time out of their busy lives to record a video to make me smile during daily radiation.

It's really hard to put into words the beautiful friendships that have been strengthened during this time. The support from strangers and counseling from groups like Ovarcome. I've also learned how sweet the little things in life are.

To experience my grandchildren's firsts and spend so much time with them each week. To feel the warmth of the sun on my skin at our favorite RV site in Port Aransas. To wake up to the sweet smell of coffee every day, thanks to my husband of thirty five years.

That life is sweet, even in the midst of the tough stuff. And that's what I'd like to remember, all the while acknowledging the difficult, painful, and long journey that this continues to be.

And here I sit today, once again going through treatment for this pesky beast. But the thing is… here I sit. With my amazing husband, beautiful daughters, darling grandkids, and friends who are everything to me.

This journey is tough and may continue to be. But I know that I am tougher because I am an Ovarcomer. And I know together we can Ovarcome.

**Lay out that
chess board.
Watch the pieces
move by themselves.
Doesn't happen.
Create your
own destiny.
Ovarcome.**

"
**Be more proactive and advocate for yourself and your health. Listen to your body.**

*- Karen Evans*

## Karen Evans

Karen was misdiagnosed multiple times, initially treated for diverticulitis and later diagnosed with IBS. Despite suffering from bowel issues, stomach pain, and persistent weight loss, Karen's concerns were overlooked until one telling day, a CAT scan revealed tumors in her ovaries.

By this time, they had also metastasized to her stomach and lungs. Upon recalling sporadic instances of diarrhea during the pandemic and a grandmother who had passed from stomach cancer, Karen was able to trace the origins of her symptoms. However, despite the trials and tribulations that always accompany a diagnosis, Karen was blessed with a strong support group of her family, therapist, and friends.

"I don't know what I would do without them," Karen says, "it's just so surreal trying to get through this mentally and physically." Karen sees hope in clinical trials, saying that she would do anything to find out where she is in her journey, where she is going with it, and how it can be made easier for the next person.

Sharing that her tumor had metastasized, and discovered it in its fourth stage, Karen recommends others to "be more proactive and not just take the answers of who is treating you.

Listen to your body," Karen says, suggesting that no family member, no friend, and even no doctor can truly know what is going on inside you.

0 in 78. Let it be
Our promise
to Ovarcome.

> Never give up. If you must, take things into your own hands and turn yourself into the ER, do it. Don't just keep waiting and waiting. They always delay. Follow your first instincts.

*- Jana Caldwell*

# Jana Caldwell

## Finding out

Jana Caldwell's ovarian cancer took a long time to be diagnosed, even when she experienced a swollen abdomen and was in a lot of pain. She was visiting a free clinic for a full year. She confided that she hadn't been able to sleep on her stomach for a long time. "I felt severe pain when I lifted things. I kept trying to get someone to help me with the tests but the financial aid took three months just to get approved for one ultrasound."

## The Journey

Jana says she just kept getting transferred from doctor to doctor at the clinic and everyone offered different advice. But essentially, she was not getting a diagnosis. Soon after, Jana decided to take matters into her own hands and turn herself into the emergency room of a different clinic. "They conducted all the tests that needed to be done within 24 hours. I was told straight away that I had ovarian cancer. I kind of expected that something was wrong. But I'm glad that I found the best gynecologist surgeon. He fixed me up."

Jana had a huge mass growing on her stomach. She did not know what it was but said she had an inkling that it may be cancer. She also felt the mass moving left or right as per her position when she was lying down at night. "Other than the pain, I did not feel any unusual symptoms at all. I did not feel overly tired. But one day I lifted a few things to the back of the truck and the next day I couldn't get up. I was in severe pain. It was happening at least once every month." Jana said when she finally took herself to the emergency room she was in acute pain and found it hard to walk.

It took approximately 11 months for Jana to be diagnosed. She shared that her gynecologist said to her "I wish we could have got this diagnosed a year ago."

# Ovarcoming

Talking about having social support from friends and family, she said, "Most of my family is away but I talk to them often. They can't give me rides but I borrow money from my mom to get gas so I can go to appointments and get prescriptions and copays. I've always feared not having money for chemotherapy. I do have a friend that I'm close to and we talk often."

Her advice to women on the same journey is, "Never give up. If you must, take things into your own hands and turn yourself into the ER, do it. Don't just keep waiting and waiting. They always delay. Follow your first instincts."

"

Facing cancer is a daunting experience. It tests you. But I've seen that having the right mindset can make a world of difference to Ovarcoming it.

- Kari Whitman

# Kari Whitman

Kari Whitman's journey with ovarian cancer began unexpectedly when she experienced a sudden acute pain attack. Recounting the incident, she said, "The pain was nothing I had ever experienced before. It was worse than labor. I had to go to the hospital. I was told that I had an ovarian torsion."

This led to a series of tests and ultimately surgery to remove both ovaries and fallopian tubes due to a cyst the doctors found inside her left ovary. While the initial tests came out clear, a pathology report revealed Clear Cell Carcinoma. Other than the torsion, Kari had no prior signs or symptoms.

She vividly recalled waking up on a Thursday morning with no inkling of the impending health challenge.

She shares that it took her only four months to go from the first check-up to diagnosis. "Another surgery was planned right after the first one to remove the uterus, cervix, a few lymph nodes, and surrounding tissues. But due to blood clot complications, surgery plans were postponed, and I was put on chemotherapy for the next five months."

Grateful for strong social support, Kari gratefully acknowledged her family and friends for assistance in appointments and household chores.

Offering advice to others facing a similar journey, she emphasized faith, positivity, and staying focused on healing, describing the experience as a roller coaster. "Facing cancer is a daunting experience. It tests you. But I've seen that having the right mindset can make a world of difference to Ovarcoming it."

Kari's positive outlook and faith remain central to her approach to Ovarcoming.

It's my life.
It's my moment.
It's my way.
It's my purpose.
It's my promise to
Ovarcome.

> **Strong emotional support like having a good friend to rely on can make a huge difference on this journey. I know it did for me.**
>
> *- Jessica Pena*

# Jessica Pena

## Finding out

A severe case of ascites, bloating, and pain took Jessica Pena to the emergency room. Her doctors drained about 19 pounds of fluid out. An ultrasound and MRI revealed some abnormalities around her uterus. Doctors recommended a hysterectomy within two months.

But before it could come to that Jessica found herself in the emergency room again. She had been feeling a burning sensation and pressure in her abdomen that made day-to-day tasks like sitting or walking much harder. On this visit, she was diagnosed with stage four ovarian cancer.

## Journey

The surgery got pushed back and Jessica did five rounds of chemotherapy. This was followed by surgery four months later and two more rounds of chemo. But Jessica attributes her relatively smooth journey of Ovarcoming to having robust social support in place.

She highlighted the unwavering presence of her best friend who visited her every Saturday after her diagnosis and how they created a "no cry zone". "She helped with everything I needed help with. We would spend amazing time together, watching movies, taking naps, or just talking. She stayed with me for hours each weekend, sometimes until two in the morning. She also threw me a surprise birthday party. Casually invited me over for dinner and when I showed up my whole family and friend circle was there. Because of her, it has been so much easier for me emotionally."

## Ovarcoming

When asked what advice she would offer to our community of women going through a similar journey, she said, "Stay 100% positive. That's what got me through all this." Jessica emphasizes the importance of staying positive and having a strong support system to help navigate the challenges of cancer diagnosis.

Jessica Pena's story is one of resilience, unexpected discoveries, and the strength derived from a supportive network. Her advice to fellow women facing similar challenges is to "not do it alone. Surround yourself with friends and family. It can be the difference between thriving and just living."

> I have been promised a future so ovarian cancer is not what's going to be the end of my story.

— Kellie Yates

## Kellie Yates

During a holiday weekend, Kellie noticed something strange. "My stomach looked like I was pregnant. I just thought maybe I was constipated," she says.

But there was something else that lay behind the unsettling situation.

After visiting the ER, Kellie was asked to get an X-ray, ultrasound, and CT scan done. It was there that the news was delivered: "The doctor came back and looked at the scans… I heard him say 'cancer,' and my mom was like 'What?' and he said, 'Yes, it's cancer.'"

After three chemos, the masses shrunk enough to be removed by surgery. Having done genetic testing, Kellie learned that both she and her daughter were positive for BRCA-1.

Despite the news, and the circumstances, Kellie was able to power through with the love and support of her mother and sister, who both cared for and looked after her. Kellie believes her story isn't over: " this is not what's going to be the end of me," she said.

Kellie encourages other women like her to live on their terms and to fight every day for their lives. She finds hope in clinical trials, saying that it would be amazing if they helped change things. "It's definitely how we learn."

Kellie conquered each day as it came to meet her, fearless in her dedication to fight what dared fight her back. "Just don't get discouraged, you know?" she says, having faith that despite her diagnosis, she had not yet finished with life.

**When nothing is certain. Anything is possible.**

> Listen to your body. If something feels different or off, don't ignore it until it's too late. Get help. The earlier you find out, the better your quality of life will be.

*- Linda Hedrick*

# Linda Hedrick

## Finding Out

The symptoms of ovarian cancer vary from person to person. For Linda Hedrick, it started with persistent pain in her lower back and hips. She sought help from her primary care physician, who recommended a transvaginal ultrasound.

The imaging revealed a concerning spot in her ovaries. Her doctor recommended that they wait it out and monitor it. In the next five months, not only did the spot grow, but Linda's CA-125 levels also rose to 1100. "Now that really got everyone's attention."

# Journey

Reflecting on the signs and symptoms, Linda recalls the persistent pain, especially during her travels. "I was traveling a lot at the time and found it harder and harder to do so. I remember I had to keep a folded jacket under me to relieve pain while on the plane. Sitting for long periods had become challenging." But despite the acute discomfort, the thought of cancer never crossed her mind. "I had no family history of cancer and even though I've worked in the healthcare sector, ovarian cancer just wasn't on my radar."

It took her a full year from the onset of symptoms to getting a diagnosis. She said she was in constant pain but it didn't have to be this way. "Listen to your body. If something feels different or off, don't ignore it until it's too late. Get help. The earlier you find out, the better your quality of life will be."

## Ovarcoming

After the diagnosis, the doctor conducted BRCA gene testing for Linda and it came out negative. She shared that it was a big relief for her daughters. Linda shared, "I have a daughter who lives in town and comes over several times a week. I have a housemate and wonderful neighbors so yes, I have a strong support system that I am very grateful for."

Linda Hedrick offers a powerful piece of advice to the community of women facing similar journeys: "Never doubt yourself. Just when you start to have that kind of discomfort, check it out and be sure. Don't delay."

Linda's journey underscores the critical importance of swift action and early detection. Her story serves as a poignant reminder to listen to our bodies, seek help promptly, and not dismiss subtle signs.

> Reach out to people, and don't be afraid to ask for help. Be strong and have faith. You will get through to the other side.

— *Latrece Lockett*

## Latrece Lockett

It was through the analysis of blood work during a cancer center screening that Latrece Lockett's ovarian cancer was discovered.

Reflecting on the signs and symptoms that led to that moment, she recalls feeling unusual pain, something she hadn't experienced before, and "a discomfort in specific areas of my body. I knew something unusual was going on with me."

Within a week or two of feeling the pain, Latrece found herself receiving her diagnosis. Luckily for her, she was able to get to the doctors and receive a diagnosis fairly quickly.

Navigating through this challenging period, Latrece acknowledges the support she receives from family and friends.

To others facing a similar path, she highlights the importance of reaching out for help and relying on faith. "If you don't have a support system, reach out to people, and don't be afraid to ask for help. Be strong and have faith. You will get through to the other side."

Just like many Ovarcomers before her, Latrece's story is one of resilience. She finds strength in faith and whatever support her loved ones can offer. Her journey underscores the need for community, faith, and a proactive approach to one's health.

On those bad days...
remember, it is okay
not to be okay.
Remember, the spirit
of Ovarcoming has
not left your side.

> Make sure you get your yearly check-ups. Life is busy and gets in the way, but don't let your health and well-being fall by the wayside.

— Marsha Cleveland

# Marsha Cleveland

## Finding Out

An ovarian cancer diagnosis came for Marsha Cleveland when she started growing a large belly despite not making any changes to her diet. She went to her ob-gyn for a check-up. "My doctor felt with her fingers and thought I needed a bowel movement. But that wasn't the case. She knew I had my uterus and ovaries taken out and said she wanted me to get a CT scan. It came back and confirmed that I had ovarian cancer."

## Journey

Reflecting on the signs and symptoms, Marsha reveals, "My stomach looked like it was about eight months pregnant, and I thought maybe I was just getting fat." The journey from symptom recognition to diagnosis was challenging.

Marsha said before the diagnosis she was rushing to the bathroom frequently and thought she had UTI and constipation. "Little did I know the tumor was sitting on my bladder and my large and small intestines, so that made it very hard for me to go to the restroom both ways."

## Ovarcoming

Supported by her family and friends, Marsha said that she has adequate social support. "My sister, nephew, and my daughter and her boyfriend are there for me emotionally and physically. I'm very blessed."

Advising women on a similar journey, Marsha emphasizes the importance of regular check-ups. "Make sure you get your yearly check-up with your ob-gyn and your general doctor. Life is busy and gets in the way, but don't let your health and well-being fall by the wayside."

**Some days the most important thing we do is the rest we take between 2 breaths, and the spirit of Ovarcoming we embrace. Keep Going. Never stop Ovarcoming!**

> Have regular check-ups and keep all your appointments so if something does happen, it can be caught early.

*- Lessie Brown*

# Lessie Brown

Lessie Brown faced her ovarian cancer diagnosis during what she thought would be a routine hysterectomy. In her own words, "I was going for a hysterectomy, and he found something that didn't look right, so they took the bloodwork. They found the mass during the surgery."

Lessie did not have any of the common and apparent symptoms of ovarian cancer. She decided to undergo a hysterectomy due to problems with persistent bleeding. Later, she was told that she had Stage 1 ovarian cancer.

Lessie is lucky to have family around to care for her; especially her daughter and husband. Her husband, who is on disability, takes her to appointments and her daughter takes care of her after the chemo sessions. "My family keeps checking on me. I'm grateful for that."

Lessie emphasized the importance of regular check-ups and screenings for those on the same path as her. She encouraged women to stay vigilant with appointments, stating, "Have regular cancer check-ups such as mammograms etc, keep all your appointments so if something does happen, it can be caught early."

Recognizing the need for emotional support, Lessie expressed interest in psycho-social counseling, stating, some days I still don't understand a lot of stuff going on with my body, and I'd like to ask questions and learn from the experience of others, I've never been like this, I've never been sick."

The journey may be challenging, but Lessie is Ovarcoming with abundant hope.

No one can
stop you from
rebounding.
No one can take
away your hope.
No one can
stop you from
rebuilding.
No one Can.

> Most importantly, stay positive. Have hope. Because hope is important in the healing process.

*- Priya Bhosale*

# Priya Bhosale

Priya Bhosale is a professional in the field of cancer, having worked in breast cancer radiology for many years. After a discussion with a friend, she realized she had not, however, had a mammogram of her own in about a decade. She decided to have one, not expecting anything particular. But she received the worst shock of her life as she read her image that showed a lump.

Priya's mind went to work and she immediately sought help. "I gathered the courage to get a biopsy. At first, I went into a dark place. I felt deformed, devastated, and sad."

It did not take her long to get a biopsy done. It took her only a month between seeing the image to getting the biopsy results. "If truth be told, my time wondering if it was contained or metastatic was extremely difficult." But she made a conscious decision to "live the month 100%".

She accepted as many invitations as possible and embraced the light. She also "meditated regularly and chanted" at the encouragement of her best friend who even held a religious ceremony on her behalf.

Priya has a tremendous circle of friends and family. Her sisters came and stayed with her during the biopsy. Her friends would come around just "to sit and watch TV" if that's what she needed. "All of this buoyed me during this period." Priya's advice to anyone on the same journey as her is this. "Do all the tests available. Mammograms. Genetic testing. If you have a family history – check it out. There is a link between breast and ovarian cancer, be sure and follow up on both. And most importantly, stay positive. Have hope. Because hope is important in the healing process."

She also believes in paying attention to your body. In hindsight, she now realizes just how tired she had felt for a long time and continued to shrug it off as nothing. "If something is different, take notice. Your body is your home. Don't take it for granted.

**Acknowledge
the sorrow behind
the silence.
Allow yourself grief.
Be patient with
yourself.
Love Yourself.**

> Don't allow cancer to become you. You are not cancer. Cancer is just a problem, a painful one, yes, but just a problem nonetheless. It can make us tired and weak, but we cannot ever let it take over who we are.

*- Linda Montgomery*

## Linda Montgomery

Linda Montgomery began to experience a few unusual symptoms after a Covid-19 diagnosis at the start of the pandemic: "I wasn't feeling better and I felt bloated… like somebody had put an air hose down my stomach and blew me up." She then went to the ER where she was diagnosed with pancreatitis and put on the pancreatitis diet.

But four weeks later, she was back at the hospital when her condition did not improve despite the changes to her diet. She visited her primary doctor who said Linda seemed to have been misdiagnosed and it did not look like pancreatitis.

She was scheduled for a CT scan and an MRI. After the results came back, Linda uncovered the truth: she had ovarian cancer.

According to Linda, while the pandemic has been uncomfortable for most people, she was grateful for the time. "My cancer was discovered by chance when I had covid and the symptoms just did not seem to get better even after a fortnight. If it wasn't for covid, I wouldn't be alive today."

Linda recalls that her tumor was initially discovered a few years ago, but was checked and left untouched by three different doctors because they said it was benign. "I told them I wasn't planning on having kids and that they should do hysterectomy. But all three refused and said they wouldn't do it without any real reason for it."

She said she is grateful for her social support. "My husband goes with me to every appointment and takes off from work just to be with me, especially for my appointments. He says if he loses his job he loses his job, I'm more important to him than anything else."

Linda also has a brother who visits often to take care of her dogs at her house and friends who showed up and decided to do a fundraiser for her. Linda was blessed with an abundance of support from family and friends. And in finding strength in them, she was able to Ovarcome.

"The number one thing is don't give up," says Linda, "don't allow the cancer to become you… we are still who we were when we got it… remember that so it doesn't take over." And it was with this mentality that Linda fought day by day to never let cancer get the best of her.

Her advice to those on a similar journey is to never give up. "Don't allow the cancer to become you. You are not cancer. Cancer is just a problem, a painful one, yes, but just a problem nonetheless. It can make us tired and weak, but we cannot ever let it take over who we are."

"

**Give yourself a chance to experience the bad days but then pull yourself up by the bootstraps and move on. Anybody who has been through this will tell you that some days are much easier than others.**

— Sally Stevens

# Sally Stevens

## Finding Out

Sally was first diagnosed with a rare type of ovarian cancer known as granulosa cell tumor in 2012. At the time of this writing, she was in active treatment for her eighth recurrence. "This cancer is so rare that I was told that it was not even cancer in 2012. The Emergency Room surgeon told me what type of tumor it was and said that it was benign - which was incorrect. I still have my discharge paperwork from the hospital. It said 'Non-Cancerous Ovarian Growth'".

## Journey

Sally experienced the usual ovarian cancer symptoms like frequent urination and early satiety. However because the granulosa cell tumor is hormonal, she gained weight and experienced facial changes like dark patches and hair growth.

"I woke up with intense abdominal pain in the middle of the night and rushed to the Emergency Room. I found out that my left ovary was ruptured with what was a softball-sized tumor."

Sally was taken for an emergency surgery. What started as a laparoscopy ended up being an open surgery when the doctor found the tumor. Along with the tumor, Sally's left ovary and a fallopian tube were also removed. "Sadly, because the doctor didn't recognize that it was cancer, she didn't do any other exploratory looking around.

When I found out in 2015 that the cancer was all over my pelvis and abdomen it made me wonder if this was a recurrence or residual disease that wasn't found in surgery in 2012?"

## Ovarcoming

As far as treatment is concerned, according to Sally, very little has worked for her thus far. The primary treatment for granulosa cell cancer is surgery and she has had eleven plus surgeries so far. Radiation worked on her once when she had a cluster of three tumors in her lower left pelvis that was inoperable due to a major vein tear during one of her recent surgeries. Other than that she tried chemotherapy, and used a multitude of different drug combinations and clinical trials, but nothing worked for her.

Despite the challenges, Sally remains in high spirits. "My family has been a huge support, especially my husband. The other thing that encouraged me to do my best was all the amazing women - other Ovarcomers - whom I met over the years. They just never cease to amaze me. The support that these women provide to each other regardless of their circumstances is unbelievable. They give you that strength even when they are struggling so much themselves."

Sally said she'd like to include her doctor in the list of people who give her immense hope and support. "He partners with me regarding my care and schedules my appointment as the last for the day because he knows it's going to take more than fifteen minutes to review a scan and talk about the possible care options. I always leave his office with plan A and then also plan B, C & D lined up."

On rough days, Sally reminds herself that it will be better tomorrow and that she just needs to make it through the day. She believes it's important not to shut out those negative feelings and give them space to be experienced and released because it is cathartic. "But you can't stay there forever.

Give yourself a chance to experience the bad days but then pull yourself up by the bootstraps and move on. Anybody who has been through this will tell you that some days are much easier than others."

Her advice to others on the same path is to hold on to hope tightly and live life fully. It's a conscious decision that everyone on this journey has to make. Cancer doesn't need to be a death sentence, she says.

It can be treated as a chronic illness. "Find your joy in every day because it's the little things that matter.

People are out there working hard for the ovarian cancer community; looking for better treatments, a cure, and trying to support other patients in every stage of their disease."

She said spreading awareness about ovarian cancer is important because it's a disease that people don't talk much about. Without awareness of the symptoms, early diagnosis is impossible. Sally believes everyone who has received a diagnosis must share personal stories and talk about BEACH symptoms as frequently as possible.

"I have awareness cards that I give out from Ovarcome. I'm not quiet about my story. I'll answer any question someone has about it. I do this because I hope by sharing a story and educating people about the symptoms, I may get someone to their doctor sooner and save a life."

> Please listen very carefully to your body. It is your biggest asset on which you build your entire life. Don't take your health for granted.

— Martha Luna

# Martha Luna

After four months of lethargy, excruciating pain in multiple areas, and strange sensations in her stomach, Martha Luna decided to take action. "My legs felt like they were going to explode," she says, "and sleeping on my tummy felt like there was something there." Martha then visited a healthcare professional, who "took the time to listen and schedule an internal ultrasound."

They found a tumor of about seven centimeters." There was one inside her ovary and another in her stomach. From the onset of symptoms to the official diagnosis, it took Martha approximately four months. After genetic testing, Martha was able to confirm that her condition "was not genetic".

She receives continued love and support from her three married sons and her "biggest support, her husband and church friends."

Knowing how difficult the journey can be, Martha offers a crucial piece of advice to others like her: "Please listen very carefully to your body. It is your biggest asset on which you build your entire life. Don't take your health for granted."

> Overall, volunteering, having a positive attitude, and praying a lot has made a difference in my life.
>
> - Susan Krell

# Susan Krell

## Finding Out

Susan Krell's journey with ovarian cancer began with a sudden and severe illness that led her to the gastroenterologist. "I just got sick," she recalls, "and the doctor told me something was wrong because I was so unwell. Then he asked me to go to the Emergency Room. I had been complaining for a long time, you know."

Over the next few months, Susan faced a series of symptoms, including a swollen abdomen, frequent urination, back pain, nausea, and an expected urinary tract issue. The path from these symptoms to a confirmed ovarian cancer diagnosis was a challenging six-month ordeal.

## Journey

Soon after her diagnosis, Susan also undertook genetic testing which came out negative. Navigating her journey with limited social support, Susan candidly admits, "I don't have a huge or supportive social circle. And that has sometimes come in the way of my well-being."

## Ovarcoming

For those traversing similar paths to Ovarcoming, Susan encourages resilience and positivity.

"I volunteered for the Ovarian Walk and Run, and that helped. But overall, having a positive attitude and praying a lot has made a difference in my life."

Your worst shot is
still pretty good.
Because you took it.
Stop chasing
to be perfect.
Become
Yourself.
No one can be
better at it.
Keep Winning.

> **Be consistent with doctor's appointments and if something doesn't feel right, get a second opinion.**
>
> *- Andrea Ramos-Murillo*

# Andrea Ramos-Murillo

Diagnosed with endometriosis, Andrea went back and forth between doctors in Mexico and the US to find a solution to her pain. Despite having visited the ER repeatedly, Andrea was not referred to a specialist. Eventually, a surgery was scheduled. When Andrea went to Mexico for surgery, the operating team discovered a large tumor blocking her intestines.

Although the tumor was removed, not all of it could be extracted. Andrea then received chemo but "the chemo… didn't work." Her cancer was of a particularly rare type, so she had to switch to a different chemo, a drug that more effectively treated her condition. "I had inflammation and sharp pain in my stomach for several years," she shared.

Andrea was the first in her family to have been diagnosed with cancer. It was not genetic.

In this journey of Ovarcoming, Andrea's family and friends were steadfastly by her side, taking her to appointments, helping around in the house, and keeping her company. It matters to have love and support, and Andrea says she is fortunate to have received both in abundance.

Andrea encourages others to "be consistent with doctor's appointments," and "if something doesn't feel right, get a second opinion." Andrea has been proactive about her health in this journey of Ovarcoming - she has persevered, and Ovarcome every challenge that has come her way with grace and confidence.

**The World Sees Your Courage, Resilience, Persistence & Faith. You Are Winners. You are Ovarcomers.**

> It is not easy for anyone. But just take it one day at a time. Take care of yourself.

— Tammy Kinard

# Tammy Kinard

## Finding out

For Tammy Kinard, the diagnosis of ovarian cancer came unexpectedly. Her journey began with a noticeable change in her abdomen which became painful and hard. Concerned, she visited the ER, where a CAT scan raised suspicions. Urgently referred to a large hospital, the news delivered was shocking. She had ovarian cancer.

## Journey

Reflecting on the signs and symptoms, Tammy shared, "I had a loss of appetite, my stomach got rock hard, I was sluggish, that was about all I experienced. I just felt run down." Despite these indicators, it took about a month for Tammy to connect the dots and seek medical attention. Unaware of the severity, she attributed her condition to relationship stress as she was not on good terms with her boyfriend.

After the shock of the diagnosis and her first chemotherapy, Tammy's support system dwindled. Her partner broke up with her and she went from having several people around to just one individual.

## Ovarcoming

Coping with the emotional toll, she humorously suggests, "I'd say run! But in all honesty, it hasn't been easy for me." Despite the challenges and unexpected turns in her journey, Tammy is moving forward with resilience, keeping humor by her side to cheer her when she needs it the most.

Tammy shares with our community of women going through ovarian cancer diagnosis or recovery:

"It is not easy for anyone. But just take it one day at a time. Take care of yourself."

We are Winners in Life. In life & after, Ovarcoming wins. Not Cancer. Always.

> **Always remember that there is a chance you can be cured.**
>
> – *Rosa Diaz*

# Rosa Diaz

Rosa Diaz experienced swollen feet, painful legs and stomach, and bloating which eventually took her to the hospital. Several hospital visits, multiple tests, and six months later she was told that she had ovarian cancer. "An eventual CT scan is what confirmed my worst fears," she said.

In Rosa's case, her cancer was not caused by hereditary factors. Luckily for her, Rosa has strong social support from her loved ones. "My son and husband live with me. They take me to all my appointments," says Rosa, "and my son cooks for me sometimes."

While navigating cancer is never easy - no matter what the individual circumstances - having support and the right mindset certainly gives people a hopeful chance.

Rosa's advice to everyone else on the same journey is to be strong. "Always remember that there is a chance you can be cured." She encourages fellow Ovarcomers to keep pushing through and have faith.

> **Keep all your appointments. Prioritize your health over everything else.**

— *Ruby Voils*

# Ruby Voils

Watching her stomach swell to the point she looked "seven months pregnant," Ruby, naturally worried about what was happening inside her body, visited the ER where they drained five liters of fluid from her stomach. "It was a very painful experience."

But just a few days after her first ER visit, her stomach continued to swell again.

Ruby revisited the hospital where the doctors told her she had an issue with her liver. She was not able to return to work for the next two weeks. After yet another set of tests, Ruby's doctors remained convinced that the issue was in her liver, though they were not sure what exactly yet. She was sent to a liver specialist who ran a few tests and confirmed that her liver was just fine, but there were some unusual spots on her ovaries.

Ruby was referred to an OB-GYN specialist, and a CT scan revealed an entirely different issue. "The doctor told me I had cancer in my ovary. After hearing the news, I was shocked and cried for a long time because I did not expect it to ever happen to me." Ruby also went through genetic testing and found that her cancer wasn't hereditary and she wouldn't be passing it down to her daughter.

"Sometimes I get depressed but I've got my husband and daughter to help me get over my issues." It is through their loving care and support that Ruby was able to power through chemo and the effects that come with it.

Ruby advises anyone on the same journey as her: "Just go and get checked every month with the doctor. Keep all your appointments. Prioritize your health over everything else."

**Ovarcoming is the life's journey best traveled with Hope.**

> **Stay positive and keep pushing forward. It's not easy but you just have to keep going.**

*- Sandra Vargas*

# Sandra Vargas

Before her ovarian cancer diagnosis, Sandra was struggling with her health: "My legs were heavy, swollen, and I was bloated... probably ten times the size it should have been," she says, "I couldn't catch my breath... and was nauseated.

When Sandra was no longer able to walk, she immediately went to the hospital. Her doctor promptly ordered a biopsy and soon, Sandra was diagnosed with ovarian cancer. Sandra was diagnosed after two months of experiencing the symptoms. To her great relief, genetic testing confirmed that her cancer was not hereditary.

"I was lucky, you know," she says. Despite the challenging circumstances, Sandra was able to push through. With family and friends to take her to appointments and with a very supportive oncologist, Sandra was able to Ovarcome. "You just need to stay positive and keep pushing forward," she says. "It's not easy, but you just have to keep going and keep Ovarcoming."

> **Learn to trust your intuition because it is a big part of recovery.**
>
> — *Yvonne Sandoval*

# Yvonne Sandoval

Having developed a severe form of ascites, Yvonne visited the ER a few times - eventually upon doing a CT scan, Yvonne discovered she had ovarian cancer. "It came as a real shock," says Yvonne, "I had been on this whole upward trajectory… and I was doing all these things that, you know, are typically beneficial for health."

She also tested positive for the BCRA-1 gene, and after her diagnosis, Yvonne received a full hysterectomy, quit her job within two weeks, and watched her mother pass away from cancer. "It was very surreal," says Yvonne.

"I'm also a single parent, the sole provider for my child, so it was just a really scary time."

Yvonne turned to her faith, praying that she would have the strength to persevere. In return, she received "this stirring message, and the message was 'you're going to live through this. It's going to be hard but you're going to know what to do.'"

It was this divine message that empowered Yvonne to persevere through her diagnosis, every complication of her chemo journey, and the ever-present challenge of staying healthy. "I'm really, really grateful that I have a network of support, or can just pick up the phone and call somebody,"

Blessed with a loving network of family and friends, Yvonne encourages other women like her to "learn to trust their intuition because it is a big part of cancer recovery."

**Let every day and every night end with a prayer for Ovarcoming.**

**"**
**Ovarcoming
is a Balancing Act.**

*- Shannon Miller*

# Shannon Miller

Shannon Miller stands as the most decorated Olympic Gymnast in United States history, boasting an impressive seven Olympic medals. She holds the unique distinction of being the only female athlete to be inducted into the US Olympic Hall of Fame not once, but twice.

In 2010, Shannon ventured into entrepreneurship by establishing her own company, dedicated to helping women prioritize their health. However, in January 2011, her life took an unexpected turn when she was diagnosed with a rare form of ovarian cancer. This pivotal moment marked the beginning of Shannon's advocacy for ovarian cancer awareness. She became committed not only to raising awareness for the cause but also to inspiring and empowering individuals to conquer their personal challenges and fostering what she aptly terms the 'Gold Medal Mindset'. Beyond her remarkable athletic and professional achievements, Shannon wears multiple hats as a devoted mother of two, a cancer survivor and Ovarcomer, an author, and a sports analyst.

We sat down with Shannon to learn about her own journey of Ovarcoming.

**Q:** In the 1996 Olympics, you made history by becoming the first American woman to win both the team gold medal and an individual gold medal. Can you share your experience with us?

**A:** It was wow! It was an incredible time and there was so much that built up to that moment. I grew up and trained in Oklahoma where my family is from and to think that my parents put me in this thing called gymnastics because I wouldn't stop jumping on the furniture and then to make it to an Olympic games where you get to represent your country on that stage is just incredible.

I moved up through the ranks just like every kid and hoped to make it to a state competition and then eventually qualify to be part of the United States National Team. I went on to participate at my first Olympics in 1992 and had the wonderful opportunity to go over to Barcelona to compete at those games.

We got on the podium as a team and won the Bronze team medal. But it felt as if we had won Gold because it was such an amazing accomplishment to break into the top three for the United States. I then came back again four years later with this incredible team now known as the Magnificent Seven. It was a dream come true moment for all of us to represent the US on home soil and have such incredible support around us.

**Q:** Tell us about your journey leading up to your diagnosis of ovarian cancer.

**A:** My journey started when I launched a women's health and wellness company in the summer of July 2010. That was before I was diagnosed. My mother is a cancer survivor. Hers wasn't a genetically related cancer but she got diagnosed in 2008.
I built the company to help women make their health a priority in every sense.

At the same time, I had also started hosting a radio show. Every weekend I would go talk to different physicians and nurses about every health topic you could possibly imagine.

As we moved into the fall we were doing a lot on cancer awareness, the importance of getting yourself examined, and making sure that's a priority.

I was starting to get a bit overwhelmed but in a good way. Things were going great at work, my schedule was packed, and our son had just turned a year old so we were celebrating all those milestones. The holidays were coming up and we were getting ready for those as well. I remember looking at my calendar one day and thinking that I was going out of town for work on the day of my next exam and did I really need to cram everything in?

I told myself that I felt fine. I'll just put it off a little bit and so I called up my doctor's office and I was completely prepared to cancel the appointment and wanted to ask for the first available appointment. When they put me on hold I had this moment where I just felt this incredible guilt about asking other women to do something that I wasn't willing to do and as they say 'walk the walk'.

When the receptionist came back on the line I said I'm going out of town on this date but maybe I can get on the first available date because I don't want to put it off for too long. She said "That's great because we just got a cancellation now and you could come over now if you want."

**Q:** What happened next?

**A:** I drove over there not even really considering my health and I certainly never thought about cancer. That morning was when they found a baseball sized cyst on my left ovary and that kind of sent me into this whirlwind of tests and scans. My doctor was fabulous.

He consulted almost immediately with a gynecologic oncologist which likely saved my life. By early January I was being scheduled for surgery. The oncologist told me that this was not going to go away on its own.

He scheduled me for surgery and I woke up to the news that it was in fact ovarian cancer.

The prognosis seemed good. They caught it early which we all know doesn't happen often enough with ovarian cancer. A couple weeks later they found out it was a higher-grade malignancy than they thought and I would need to go through a pretty aggressive chemotherapy regimen. That's the point where my mentality changed.

I went from the mentality that everything was happening to me and I had no control over anything to that competitive mentality I had known through sport. I told myself that okay we know what we're dealing with now. We can create a plan of action. It's not going to be easy, but what's easy?

Nothing's easy so let's attack it. I'm going to get chemo, hey I'm an Olympic gold medalist, I can do this. I kept giving myself all these pep talks. I think chemo was really a lot tougher than I ever imagined. Every woman out there, every person that has gone through this whether you've gone through it as a survivor or as a caregiver, you understand how difficult the journey can be.

**Q:** What were the signs and symptoms that you experienced?

**A:** I went for my checkups thinking I felt completely fine. But my husband reminded me. He said 'Shannon do you remember calling me at work? You were doubled over with stomach pains and you were worried because you weren't sure if you were going to be able to lift our son out of his crib when he was finished with his nap' and I had completely forgotten about this incident.

Because I think we often put our health on the back burner. As soon as it's over we're onto the next thing. For me, that was a real eye opener. I also realized that I didn't know what the signs and symptoms of ovarian cancer were.

It's really easy for me to say I didn't have them if I don't know what they are. Looking back, I did. I had three of the four major symptoms.

I had stomach pains and bloating. I remember going to a very important business meeting and I got my best suit, my favorite suit, my lucky suit to put on and I remember realizing that I lost six pounds in about a month's span but I thought I'm losing baby weight. But I still couldn't zip the skirt up.

I was bloated and for most women it's so easy to overlook. The signs are so generic so it's difficult to signal there's something really wrong. But if you have these signs and they are lasting more than two weeks, go see a doctor.

**Q:** How was your mindset at that time?

**A:** I learned to thrive because of other women who helped me including the medical staff, friends, family, or neighbors. What also helped was listening to the inspiring stories of Ovarcomers and their family members who reached out to me. It helped me realize I wasn't alone.

This journey can be very isolating. And I'm so thankful and feel so blessed for so many who were willing to share their story with me. That was one of the big reasons I felt like I had to share my story with everyone because it is so important and you never know whose life you are going to touch, what little nugget they're going to be able to take with them that will help them thrive in the journey.

For me, relying on lessons learned through sport was a big one and so was goal setting. But goal setting for me was not about learning a big skill or winning a gold medal, it was about walking twice around my dining room table. And most days, that was my big goal, if I can get dressed, and I can walk two times around our dining room table which is not large, that was a good day for me, and I could kind of check the box.

Teamwork is so essential. It's important to realize that you have this incredible team around you. Not just the medical staff that's supporting you but also friends, family, neighbors, coworkers who are making it easier everyday.

The understanding that I was part of that team enabled me to step up and really make sure I was contributing each step of the way. When we know that others are depending on us, that's where we thrive, especially as women because we are always there for everybody else and yet somehow we're not there for ourselves. So if we can start looking at it as a team then it's a little bit easier to make our health a priority. Other things that helped me are positive attitude and having faith and understanding that if I get this day then I'm going to make the most of it. Yes, they're not all going to be great and they're not all going to be cheery but I believe that a positive attitude is about finding gratitude.

**Q:** How do you support others on this journey?

**A:** There's never anything too small that we can do. I'm grateful for the opportunity to be here and utilize the platform I've created from my Olympics career to help others. Creating awareness by speaking up and speaking out is incredible.

I know I have a certain skill set, I am not going to find a cure for cancer, (though I'd love to), but I can certainly help people in other ways. I can highlight the importance of funding for research via these platforms, help create awareness about the signs and symptoms, and make sure that all women, anyone with ovaries, should know the signs and symptoms associated with ovarian cancer. That also means getting the men involved because they all have wives, daughters, mothers, sisters, and cousins. So, it's not really just a women's disease, it is about the whole family unit.

**Q:** What's your message to others on this journey?

**A:** There were moments where I did not feel like myself at all. Going from winning the olympics to not being able to open a water bottle, it can kind of mess you up. My mother really helped me through this time because she had gone through a very difficult battle with cervical cancer.

She underwent radiation, chemotherapy, and surgery and at one point she was down to 86 pounds. She understood everything that I was going through. She told me 'look, you just need to take some time. You don't have to get worked up and you don't have to push yourself.

Don't drive yourself crazy by trying to create these big goals. Just take it one day at a time. Do the best you can.' and that really stuck with me.

And now I tell everyone that don't assume you're going to feel 100% three months after chemo or even six months. It may even take a full year but just understand that it's a process. Once I got my mind around the idea and I could equate that to my Olympic journey.

That one gold medal moment lasted like a minute. The journey lasted a lot longer and I'm thankful for that journey because I learned so many lessons. That's the same thing with cancer. It's a journey that has good days and bad days. But I learned a lot of lessons during this time and I think I came out stronger for it. I've seen one thing in common with all cancer survivors; we are so much stronger than we ever imagined we could be.

We are all in different stages in their journey. I love the word thrive rather than survive because we are not just surviving, we're not just getting by, we are finding those ways to thrive and they don't always have to be big and grand. The fact is it's in the small moments and in those small victories that we really do make that big difference along the way.

So my message today is to just keep taking that next forward step. Today might be a great day or it might be a really tough day. Just take the next forward step and that's all you need to do. Take that next forward step and remember that you have an incredible team and support system around you.

If you don't, then there are amazing people and organizations out there like Ovarcome that are available to you for support. I'm so appreciative to those that reached out and helped me during that tough phase. I know that all of us in turn at some point can reach out and help someone else.

"It's a balancing act. Keep Ovarcoming."

# The Light shines on

## Ovarcoming doesn't end when life does.

# Ovarcoming
# Leaving a legacy

## Stories of Support in Spirit

Release your shadows.
Rebuild the lost.
Reflect on lessons.
Remember the good.
Rejoice in the lessings.
Recharge your spirit of Ovarcoming.

# Sherry Pollox

Sherry Pollex was diagnosed with ovarian cancer at the age of 35 and was widely recognized not just for her celebrity status but for how she helped guide, educate, and inspired thousands of ovarian and childhood cancer patients and survivors. She championed several cancer-related causes dedicated to raising awareness and funds for cancer patients.

She also created SherryStrong.Org to help individuals with ovarian cancer get early detection and know the best treatment options available to them. Her Sherry Strong Integrative Medicine Oncology Clinic was designed as a holistic center to support cancer patients with their physical, emotional, and spiritual needs. Sherry passed away at 44 after 9 years of being diagnosed with ovarian cancer. Her story stands as a testament to the transformative power of maintaining a positive outlook and supporting others even in the most challenging times.

The following interview was conducted with Sherry Pollex in 2020, 6 years after she was diagnosed with ovarian cancer.

**Q:** You were diagnosed with stage three ovarian cancer at 35. Could you share the symptoms and signs you encountered, and how you ultimately received your diagnosis?

**A:** I experienced the typical symptoms of bloating, pelvic pain, frequent urination, lower back pain, and changes in bowel habits – a combination familiar to many ovarian cancer patients. The challenge lies in these symptoms being common and often attributed to other factors like menopause, PMS, or just having a bad day honestly. For me, these persisted for about two months, and that's when I started consulting various doctors. Unfortunately, I underwent the typical patient pinball process, bouncing between diagnoses like Crohn's disease, colitis, and irritable bowel syndrome.

Throughout this journey, no one mentioned ovarian cancer, and I wasn't aware of it being a possibility at my age.

Even during visits to my ob-gyn, where ovarian cysts were identified through ultrasounds, the topic of ovarian cancer never came up. With no family history and being seemingly healthy, it never crossed our minds.

This lack of awareness extends to the medical system. Doctors seldom consider ovarian cancer in younger women, and routine questions about family history are often missed. Despite warning signs and my mother later being diagnosed with breast cancer during my chemotherapy, the dialogue about ovarian cancer remained absent.

As an advocate now, I've encountered numerous women, even younger than me, diagnosed at late stages. Changing this narrative involves pushing for an early detection test, raising awareness among doctors about the age range for this disease, and empowering women to communicate effectively with their healthcare providers.

The breakthrough in communication within our medical system is crucial for improving survival rates.

**Q:** You mentioned your mom; does that mean you have a genetic history or a family history of cancer?

**A:** I underwent testing for the BRCA gene during my initial chemotherapy, and the results were negative. Neither my mom nor my sister carries the gene. Luckily, my mom, diagnosed at stage one, opted for a lumpectomy and radiation, which is a common path for stage 1 breast cancer patients. Unfortunately, this is less typical for ovarian cancer cases.

Despite being BRCA negative initially, my tumor later mutated to become BRCA positive. It's an unexpected twist, but in the context of my recurrence, being BRCA-positive has enhanced my treatment efficacy.

**Q:** What challenges have you faced in your journey with ovarian cancer?

**A:** The primary challenge is the scarcity of young women with ovarian cancer, and even among those, some may prefer to move on after their treatment without speaking about their experience.

While I respect and understand their choice, I believe there's a crucial need for more young voices to stand up and share their stories. It's essential to convey that this disease can affect anyone, regardless of age or health status.

Undoubtedly, funding is a significant hurdle. Securing better funding from institutions and government programs is crucial, and I'm pleased to see progress in this area. Advocating for early detection tests has also been a major challenge.

Moreover, the broader challenge lies in getting timely diagnosis from doctors. Even with or without an early detection test, convincing doctors to consider the possibility of ovarian cancer in young women with seemingly common symptoms remains an ongoing struggle.

On a personal level, I faced challenges like many others-losing my hair, struggling with physical limitations, and contending with the emotional toll.

However, I consciously shifted my mindset towards focusing on positive aspects of my life during that difficult period. I recognized it as a temporary season in my life.

I embraced the idea of living well with cancer, treating it more like a chronic illness than a death sentence. This mindset shift has been powerful in managing the disease, allowing me to lead a fulfilling life since my diagnosis in 2014.

**Q:** What is the one regret that you have and how have you turned it into a strength?

**A:** One regret I have in my cancer journey, particularly at the time of my diagnosis, revolves around how I initially sought information. When I learned about my stage three ovarian cancer diagnosis, I turned to the internet, thinking it would be a source of valuable information.

However, the reality is that the internet, especially when it comes to cancer information, can be a scary place. The content is often outdated, and it can instill fear.

When I Googled my diagnosis and came across statistics and information, I panicked. I texted my doctor and asked him if he had given me a death sentence? He texted back saying: 'Stay off the internet.' He explained that many patients react this way after leaving his office, overwhelmed by the kind of information that's available online.

What I've learned and often share with others is the importance of understanding that we are unique individuals and that our cancer journey is highly personal. Comparing our stories to others can be like comparing apples to oranges. We don't share the same DNA, cancer type, stage, or classification. We respond differently to treatments because our situations are inherently distinct.

Engaging with other survivors can be valuable for sharing experiences and seeking advice. It's okay to inquire about their journey, treatments that worked for them, or any insights they can offer. However, it's crucial not to equate their path with ours. What worked for someone else may not necessarily be the best approach for us.

Instead, the information gained from others should be used as a basis for asking our oncologists personalized questions and making informed decisions.

I wish I'd known this from the start. Now, when I speak at hospitals or in front of fellow cancer patients, I tell them to avoid "Doctor Google." The internet can be overwhelming and may not always provide accurate or helpful information. This one change can significantly contribute to a more positive and empowered approach to facing the challenges at hand.

**Q:** What is the one message that you would give to a fellow survivor who just got diagnosed or is going through treatment and is in fear of the cancer coming back?

**A:** Reflecting on my past, I wish I could go back and advise my younger self, the scared girl facing an ovarian cancer diagnosis that yes, the cancer can come back but that doesn't mean you should spend every single waking hour worrying about it.

Dwelling on the fear of recurrence wouldn't change the outcome. But when in remission, it's your chance to make beautiful memories with your friends and family, instead of living in fear. My advice to fellow ovarian cancer patients is to acknowledge the possibility of recurrence but not to expect it. Worrying daily about a potential relapse is mentally taxing. Instead, focus on living each day fully. No amount of worry changes the outcome, and it's crucial to remember that.

There's no magic cure or guarantee against the recurrence of any cancer. Ovarian cancer does have a higher recurrence rate, but effective drugs are available to combat it.

When faced with a recurrence, my approach was clear. I underwent a PET scan, opted for surgery, and engaged in testing to identify the most suitable chemotherapy drugs. I emphasize the importance of proactive measures – understanding your body's response to drugs, seeking personalized advice, and formulating a strategy to navigate through chemotherapy. Having faced a recurrence, the goal became returning to remission.

There's immense hope out there, but many survivors aren't actively sharing their stories online. They're out, living their lives, making memories, and not dwelling on cancer. It's crucial to follow individuals who bring positivity and focus on the joy of living.

When speaking to cancer patients, I stress the importance of controlling what you can: your attitude, nutrition, exercise, and overall positivity. These factors contribute significantly to overall well-being. On a lighter note, if I were a crayon, I'd be lavender. I adore the color and find the scent of lavender calming.

My inner sparkle comes from daily efforts to maintain a positive mindset, influenced by my upbringing and the joy-inducing activities I engage in. Surrounding myself with positivity and spreading happiness is a continuous goal. Also limiting exposure to distressing news, spending time outdoors, and focusing on positive accounts on social media can help alleviate anxiety so common in cancer patients. It helped me a lot.

**Q:** What would be your parting message to our survivors and Ovarcomers?

**A:** The remarkable progress we've witnessed in new drugs is a beacon of hope for ovarian cancer patients. Looking back at the past five years, we've experienced a significant shift in the landscape of chemotherapy medicines for ovarian cancer. In the era of Gilda Radner, back in the eighties, treatment options remained relatively stagnant. However, today, we are witnessing the emergence of groundbreaking drugs - the strides we've made are nothing short of extraordinary

Therefore, maintaining hope and anticipation for the next medical breakthrough is crucial. I'm dedicated to empowering women; every patient needs to stay positive and anticipate these imminent medical advancements. It's a future filled with hope, and we need to focus on that.

Sherry bid us farewell, but her powerful message of hope and Ovarcoming will linger in our hearts forever.

> I have come to believe no one is to blame for my cancer, least of all me. It's happening to me, like a turn in the road on this journey I call my life.

— *Louise Smith*

# Louise Smith

## Finding Out

Louise Smith was diagnosed with Ovarian Cancer stage IVa in late September 2020. But her story started long before that. She had relocated to Portland, Oregon, from a small rural town in the late summer of 2019. She married the love of her life - reunited after 30 years - and retired from a career in Emergency Medical Services.

Her husband was diagnosed with a rapidly progressing form of ALS in May 2018. Louise traveled to Portland weekly for a year to be with him for a few days at a time and their bond grew.

By the time they married in July of 2019, he was on a ventilator full time, had no use of his hands or legs, was confined to a bed, and relied on a feeding tube for nutrition.

He was in a Veteran Administration care facility and they allowed Louise, at his insistence, to help with his care. Louise spent 10-12 hour days with him, 7 days a week once she relocated to Portland. She felt sad to notice that his friends had stopped visiting, except for his two oldest friends.

"It's hard to watch a vibrant, healthy person wither into a sick person with a debilitating disease.

When the pandemic hit, my husband's facility was shut down to visitors. Thankfully, they reclassified me as a caregiver and I was able to continue my daily routine with twice-weekly Covid testing.

Needless to say, this was very stressful for everyone, the staff, myself, and my husband. He was now unable to communicate and could not even move his eyes."

## The Journey

That summer, Louise started to have some of the B.E.A.C.H. symptoms so common in ovarian cancer. But she did not think much of them until she started having consistent pain. She started to bloat and her appetite changed, and so did her bowel movements. "I thought I was constipated or had a bowel obstruction. I was very fatigued. I didn't have a primary care doctor so I had to wait a month to establish myself with one."

Basic blood work, an EKG, and a physical exam later, Louise's doctor still had no clue what was going on. At this point, Louise suggested that the doctor allow her to go for an abdominal CT scan because she felt there was fluid in her abdomen. He reluctantly agreed. "When the report came in from my CT, I read it and knew immediately it was not good. What transpired in the next 3 weeks was a whirlwind of events. I established care with a gynecological oncologist. I felt secure with her and that I was a part of "the team" needed to go up against this cancer."

## Ovarcoming

Louise's doctor drained the fluid from her abdomen and lung area and she was scheduled for her first chemotherapy "I was going through all this and still seeing my husband as much as I could every day." When Louise's chemo started, she needed more rest, especially right after each procedure. But she was right back at caring for her husband until she had her debulking surgery.

What was supposed to be a four-hour surgery ended up being an eight-hour procedure and an ileostomy.

"It's very strange to look down at your abdomen and see the surgical staples - from the bottom of my breast bone to my pelvic bone along with a bag for solid waste elimination. It took me a few days to feel the gravity of my situation."

Louise spent 16 long days in the hospital and another week before she was able to see her husband again. Louise had home help coming in to change her ileostomy and work on her surgical wound. "Sometimes, the ileostomy would come apart in the middle of the night and there'd be a mess everywhere. But the nurse would come and put me back together again. It was not easy."

While at a wound care clinic visit, she received a call that her husband was not doing well and that she should come immediately. Louise knew his time was nearing the end and she had promised to be there for him, holding his hand, no matter what. "And I did that. But suddenly, I had a huge hole in my life. All this time that I spent daily with my husband was over. I was completely overwhelmed with emotion about his death and my disease."

Louise said she was lucky to find a therapist who helped her develop a new routine in her life. She helped Louise understand what she was going through emotionally and that it was going to feel overwhelming at times.

"It was around this time that I found Ovarcome and the Teal Truth Online Group Counseling meetings. Immediately, I felt I had found my people - people who understood what I was going through with my body, mind, and spirit. It was a safe space where I could talk freely about the physical challenges I was having and about the emotions I was experiencing. Being there was like getting a huge hug."

As an Ovarcomer in her third year at the time of this writing, Louise said she had learned a few things that have helped her stay focused and balanced. "First, I started looking at my cancer as a chronic disease, something that I have to live with, adjusting my life accordingly.

My part in the treatment included monitoring my side effects and letting my care team know what was going on. I learned to ask for help with things around my home. This is something I'm still not good at. I found a support system with Ovarcome and with others locally who are on a similar journey.

I'm making new friends. I have come to believe it is vital to do fun things and make plans for concerts, dinners, and overnight getaways. I also took care of my end-of-life decisions and arrangements, not wanting to leave my family wondering and having to deal with it all after the fact.

Most of all, I have come to believe no one is to blame for my cancer, least of all me. It's happening to me, like a turn in the road on this journey I call my life."

Louise took her last turn in the journey, to be free and to Ovarcome all the pain and anguish of this disease. She is smiling down upon you as you read this…..her words.

She wants you to keep Ovarcoming.

**No matter where we are in the journey of Ovarcoming, we Ovarcome together.**

# Nadia Chaudhuri

## May 1, 2021

Dear Runsi

Thank you for contacting me. I am honored by this invitation and am happy to accept it. Maybe we can plan for this in a couple of weeks after I've recovered from yesterday's chemo? Until then, please send me whatever additional details you think may be relevant.

Best wishes
Nadia

## May 27, 2021

Hi Runsi

Thanks for getting in touch. I've been in an out of hospital with bowel obstruction and starting a new chemo tomorrow. Let's plan touch base next week.

Thanks
Nadia

Dr. Chaudhri wrote to Runsi, Ovarcome's Founder.

The conversation did not happen as Dr. Chaudhuri's health took an abrupt but expected turn. Her light shines on brighter each day and reminds us of the work that lies ahead of us in raising awareness on Ovarian Cancer and sharing the **B.E.A.C.H.** symptoms far and wide so every woman and family knows about it, shares it, and empowers one another.

Nadia Chaudhri, a world-renowned neuroscientist, passed away from ovarian cancer at 43. Dr. Chaudhri in her life, as well in her death, was a true Ovarcomer. She embraced both with love, courage, and acceptance.

In the end, she was ready to Ovarcome life with grace, and with a promise for a feast at her forest table. She was you. She was us. She was every woman. Her life and after is a true testament of Ovarcoming.

Let's continue to carry on her legacy by empowering every woman and family with information about Ovarian Cancer. Share the **B.E.A.C.H.** Symptoms:

B = Bloating

E = Early Satiety or feeling full quickly

A = Abdominal and/or Pelvic Pain

C = Changes in Bowel/Bladder Habits

H = Heightened Fatigue

Her words. Her Message of Ovarcoming:

In January 2020 I started feeling unwell. I was tired, had vague abdominal pain, severe lower back pain & a mild increase in frequency to urinate.

I was treated with antibiotics for a UTI even though I did not have classic UTI symptoms (high bacterial load, burning pee, big increase in urge to pee).

I also got an endovaginal ultrasound that showed free fluid in the abdomen & the possibility of a ruptured left ovarian cyst. The recommendation was to follow up in 3 months.

Antibiotics plus a laxative seemed to treat my ailments. But then by mid-February all the symptoms returned. My doctor prescribed a different course of antibiotics, although again in the absence of classic UTI symptoms. Things seemed to improve a bit.

Come March, the pandemic struck. By now my abdomen was bloated and I was in moderate pain. My bowel movements had changed too so I kept taking stool softeners. I couldn't see my doctor because of the pandemic. I was incredibly tired, but I chalked it up to the pandemic.

By April I was on a third course of antibiotics. My doctor still suspected an ailment related to my urinary tract. I was tired but thought it was the antibiotics.

In May I had a second endovaginal ultrasound. This one showed that my ovaries were enlarged and had moved towards the middle of my abdomen. There was a lot of ascites in my abdomen too. The radiologist suggested endometriosis.

I showed my scan report to an Uncle who is a gynecologist. He said I should get a blood test to check CA 125, CA 19 and CEA. These are cancer markers. He wanted to rule them out before pursuing endometriosis as an option. My CA 125 came back at 925. The normal level is 0-35.

The next day I had an endovaginal ultrasound, followed by a CT scan and blood work. Four days later I met my Doctor in her in clinic. She said 24 of 25 doctors in the tumor board said I had cancer. She was holding out for endometriosis.

Two weeks later I had a laparotomy. They cut me open from sternum to pubic bone. Indeed, I had cancer. They removed all of the visible disease in a four-hour surgery. It happened on June 10, 2020. About 6 months after I first started 'feeling bad.'

4 weeks later I began chemotherapy. Standard of care for ovarian cancer has not changed in 30 years. My CA 125 dropped, a good sign.

I was also enrolled in a clinical trial that began on cycle 2 of chemotherapy.

Then in mid-December my CA 125 started to creep up. Not a good sign. It crept up slowly. But because this started happening within 6 months of the end of chemo it meant that my cancer had a label: platinum resistant. It had learned to evade the platinum-based chemo.

I remained on the clinical trial until March when I developed a bowel obstruction. This disqualified me from the trial.

Between March and now I've had more bowel obstructions than I care to count. The most recent one hasn't opened. It is why I have moved to palliative care. I can't poop or pass gas. I can't eat. I've been on IV fluids for 2 weeks.

My official diagnosis is high grade serus epithelial, platinum resistant ovarian cancer.

The bottom line is that ovarian cancer research is underfunded. We also need more awareness of symptoms because early detection improves prognosis dramatically.

I hope you found this thread helpful. Know your bodies. Pay attention to fatigue and changes in bowel or urinary tract movements. Make sure you understand all the words on a medical report.

Do not dismiss your pain or malaise. Find the expert doctors.

Although this has been the most frightening time of my life, it has been filled with brightness and love.

I have never felt so much love. I have built legacies through the immense generosity of family, friends and a tribe of supporters who have bolstered me into the clouds.

I will feast in my new life and welcome everyone to my forest table.

I am not afraid."

Thousand chances to count the odds and read facts. One chance to live and to Ovarcome.

> You are not alone. We Ovarcome together, as we walk hand in hand, toward hope.

When you fall off a cliff,
you feel the rush of adrenaline,
the air knocked out of you
your mind in dismay,
and yet, you always think
yourself out of a jam,
out of a cliff,
out of a crash,
into Ovarcoming.


You heal
when you recover from the scars,
you Ovarcome
when the scars
no longer control you.

Many have walked the path of Overcoming before you, are walking with you, or will be walking after you. No matter where you are in the journey of Overcoming, love, hope, and community surround you. Ovarian cancer diagnosis can be isolating.

But we are here for you - every step of the way, as we have been, for everyone diagnosed. We are Ovarcome - a local, national, global ovarian cancer foundation created to support, love, and assist all Ovarcomers as they go through this journey of Overcoming.

We are here for all Caregivers that stand by the Ovarcomers with their unwavering love; giving themselves fully and helping ease the burden of diagnosis.

Ovarcome has helped millions worldwide with awareness, education, and support. It was founded to give the gift of the spirit of Overcoming to all diagnosed with ovarian cancer - the spirit that we all hold closest to our hearts.

Ovarcome is spelled with an "a" to acknowledge Ovarcoming ovarian cancer, and to uphold the true spirit and intention of the word.

We are Ovarcome - we believe in love, support, advocacy, commitment to cure, and hope. We are your friend, and we will be with you when you need us, in or beyond the pages of this book - always.

Amanda Wallace is a social worker who was diagnosed with advanced ovarian cancer a few years ago. She shares her journey of Ovarcoming and how Ovarcome has been the beacon of hope she has been searching for since her diagnosis.

Q: What was your initial reaction when you received the diagnosis?

A: I was initially terrified, but my incredible support system immediately reminded me that I could survive and beat it and that really helped.

Q: Can you describe the journey of your treatment and the support you received?

A: I began treatment with chemotherapy. Ovarcome's chemo gift bag really helped lift my spirits along with the financial assistance I received from them, along with being introduced to a network that could provide me with a lot of support throughout my journey.

Q: What were the most challenging aspects of your cancer journey, and how did you navigate them?

A: The most difficult aspects for me were the side effects, I had really bad body aches but my friends made sure to keep me active and busy.

Q: Were there specific strategies that helped you stay positive during challenging times?

A: When I would get down or feel overwhelmed, I would share my thoughts and emotions on my social media, and the support from friends and family always lifted me back up. It was overwhelming at times to see how much support I received just for sharing my story.

Q: How did the support from Ovarcome impact your emotional and physical well-being?

A: It played a huge role in educating me more about the disease which not only gave me more confidence emotionally but physically I learned what things I could be doing to help navigate the disease. They really provide you with everything you need to successfully manage the disease.

Q: Were there other support networks or individuals who played a crucial role in your recovery?

A: My family was a huge part as well. They really went above and beyond to make sure I was never alone and always had support to ovarcome.

Q: What changes or perspectives did ovarcoming ovarian cancer bring to your life?

A: It made me more outspoken and eager to accomplish all the things I've wanted to do but was too scared to do. It also made me want to be an advocate and really speak out about the horrible disease.

Q: Can you share some of the positive aspects or new opportunities that emerged post-recovery?

**A:** I have had the privilege of sharing my story through Ovarcome which has been an amazing experience.

**Q:** If you could advise someone currently battling ovarian cancer, what would it be?

**A:** Don't ever give up, stay positive, you are stronger than you think and can and will Ovarcome.

**Q:** How has your perspective on life changed since ovarcoming this challenge?

**A:** I'm more positive and I no longer take life for granted. I don't waste time on little things that don't matter and I just try to enjoy life.

**Q:** In what ways did Ovarcome contribute to your recovery journey?

**A:** Ovarcome played a huge role from the beginning. From the initial gift bag and financial grant, to conferences that provided me with important information, to a network of other survivors I could share my experiences with. It kept me lifted and reminded me I wasn't alone.

**Q:** Are there specific programs or initiatives from Ovarcome that stood out in supporting you?

**A:** The conferences hosted by Ovarcome are my favorite as they cover so many things. Having both Ovarcomer and doctors sharing information as well as networking with other current patients always helps me broaden my knowledge and gives me hope.

**Q:** How do you hope your story will inspire and support others facing similar challenges?

**A:** I hope it reminds them that there is support out there and that they are not alone. I want them to know that they are strong, beautiful, Ovarcomers!

Yes you are! We invite you to lend your powerful voice to ovarian cancer awareness and to embrace the spirit of Ovarcoming as you walk this path purposefully, with the conviction to Ovarcome.

Share the **B.E.A.CH.** symptoms of ovarian cancer:

B = Bloating

E = Early Satiety or feeling full quickly

A = Abdominal &/or Pelvic Pain

C = Changes in Bowel/Bladder Habits

H = Heightened Fatigue

Become our friend on social media, attend our events, conferences and empowerment sessions. Join us for our group counseling sessions. Visit our website to learn about all the programs and services we offer.

From financial, psycho-social, and informational assistance to knowledge and information, we are here to empower you as you navigate this journey as a true Ovarcomer.

Every new day is another chance to Ovarcome - seize it.

Exhale fear, inhale courage, seek support, stand strong, give thanks, live life, make memories, nurture hope, embrace love, shine your light and always choose Ovarcoming!

Keep giving the gift of love abundantly. Because for you, someone still hopes, someone still fights, and someone still Ovarcomes.

# Ovarcoming Loss with love

## Stories of Support

Keep the
quiet light of
Ovarcoming
burning in
your heart.

# Mike Bradbury

Being a caregiver encompasses many things, but I believe the most important is the support you give. It's sitting in waiting rooms, long drives back and forth to the hospital, a second set of eyes and ears, a hand to hold or a shoulder to cry on.

My wife, Rachel, was diagnosed with Breast and Ovarian cancer at the young age of 41. Of the two, the ovarian cancer was the more serious because it was stage IIIC. Rachel was also positive for BRCA1 which went undiscovered until this diagnosis. We had three young children and this newfound diagnosis put a lot on our plates. Literally overnight our world changed and would never be the same.

During the initial diagnosis it felt like we were living at the hospital with endless doctor visits, tests, procedures, biopsies and everything in between. It happened so fast and seemed so surreal as if we were in a movie and we quickly went from going about our normal daily routine to dealing with a very serious disease. Rachel started chemotherapy as soon as possible. The first time I watched, as they injected it into her body, all I could think about was, "is this really happening?"

Just like Rachel's life had changed drastically mine did as well. As a husband and a caregiver my primary focus was on Rachel's health and getting her the necessary treatment she needed. It was extremely In addition, we still had three children at home to take care of and navigate their journey as well.

After she recovered from the ovarian cancer treatments, Rachel started on breast cancer treatments. Over thirteen long months since her initial diagnosis, she had completed her treatments and was considered NED or no evidence of disease. One special moment was surprising her on her last day of radiation along with some of Rachel's close friends. We watched as she rang the bell signifying her completion of treatment and celebrated with a fun lunch. Life felt almost normal again.

We tried to go on about life as best we could. We joined support groups, raised money for cancer research, wrote articles to educate the public about ovarian cancer. We lived every day to its fullest, enjoyed every minute with our children, attended concerts and trips we would normally have put off until later, loved more deeply, established stronger relationships with friends and family, and were more grateful than ever to be alive!

After about two years Rachel had her first recurrence. After fifteen months on the new treatment, Rachel had her second recurrence. This time we decided to try a Clinical trial.

During the trial period Rachel started to build fluid in her pleural cavity. In addition to all the other treatments she was dealing with we now had to drain this fluid daily. My nursing skills had improved, and I was able to perform these drains at home which saved many trips to the hospital. Rachel would get anxious and only felt comfortable with me performing the drain. Even if the nurses were around, she would only want me to handle the draining. In a strange way this became a special bonding time for us and it was my way to show her my love.

In March 2021, Rachel was diagnosed with MDS (Myelodysplastic syndromes that further complicated her condition. Her body simply couldn't take anymore treatment. There were countless days and nights where she just couldn't get out of bed. There were many medications to treat the side effects. As a caregiver, it was comforting to just be there and accompany her to all of the doctor visits, the hospital stays and the trips back and forth. Having someone with you can ease some of the anxiety and stress.

In September of 2021, Rachel's condition took a turn for the worse. Her cancer had spread to her lungs. After a three day hospital stay she was able to come home, but she needed oxygen. She had severe shortness of breath and after only a week we were back to the hospital where we stayed for seven days. The doctors informed us that there was nothing more they could do.

We made the difficult decision to come home on hospice care. Initially, we didn't think she would be able to be at home since she was on high flow oxygen. However, with the help of some medication we were blessed that her condition stabilized enough to come home. My sister and aunt are both nurses and flew down from Boston to help care for Rachel. We spent her remaining time at home making sure she was as comfortable as possible. During this time it was very difficult and stressful as we knew her condition was deteriorating. However, it was so nice to have her home, instead of being stuck in a hospital. Rachel was able to spend her last days with the children, family and friends.

The night before Rachel passed, we were up all night. She just couldn't settle, and her body was starting to shut down. It was the longest night of my life. I just tried to calm her and hold her hand and tell her everything was going to be okay. The morphine was helping to mask the pain. As the morning progressed her breathing became less and less. As I was holding her hand, Rachel took her last breaths. As much as I wanted her not to leave us, she would no longer have to suffer or be in pain.

My caregiver days were over. She fought so bravely, and her grace and beauty were unmatched. The thought of death was something Rachel had to deal with for many years. She prepared our family well and made sure we were going to be okay. The children will always have her love and support and know their mother was the absolute best. She showed us with grace and beauty what it means to be a true champion in life.

It was the honor of my life to take care of Rachel during her illness. I wish I could have done more, but that is the toughest part about cancer and being a caregiver. I will love her forever.

In memory of Sweet Baby Rae,
**Mike Bradbury**

Care considers.
Love lingers.
Hope heals.
Ovarcoming
triumphs.

## Jason Rosenthal

Try each day to think of one thing you feel grateful for, and I promise you, you will find something. Enjoy the unexpected time you get with the ones you love.

We were looking forward to this phase in our lives. The day, the very day she called me complaining about her stomach pain, my wife Amy was returning from a business trip. We had recently become empty nesters with the youngest of our three children just gone off to college.

She was on a business trip when she first felt the discomfort – Amy was a very strong woman who rarely ever complained of health issues. I actually took her to the ER straight from the airport – this is when we found out that she had something serious brewing that needed further attention that turned out to be very aggressive late stage ovarian cancer.

Amy didn't like the word battle. When she was diagnosed, we were still hopeful about her outcome. We were hyper focused on getting Amy better. Through the treatment, we had a very brief moment where we thought she was in remission. It was summer, we threw a party, and we danced the night away at our house – she looked amazing in her cute jumpsuit. That lasted for a very brief period, we went to the doctor shortly thereafter as her cancer had returned. The future didn't look too bright. Regardless of how bleak the outcome is, remember who the patient is and their connection to you. All I could think about is making Amy comfortable and showering her with the love which only grew stronger during that time. That's all I lived for.

We decided on home hospice and infused our lives with music because she was a music enthusiast. I brought in live musicians of every genre – it was such a meaningful experience. I showered our home with candles, and even started making my own candles – it spoke to me. It is hard being a caregiver. For me, it was almost, I didn't even feel that until Amy was gone. There is a tremendous amount of self-sacrifice in being a caregiver. I had to go back to work, take care of Amy, oversee the well-being of my children – it was compounding. You do have to try a little bit to take care of yourself too.

It is a complicated mission to do home hospice, but for me I had the instinct that that's where Amy would be most comfortable and where we could best orchestrate the final chapter of our lives; to have her experience comfort, family, friends, memories, beauty and hope as much as possible. Home hospice also prepared me to cope with the loss my dog, my dad and my dad-in-law within two years of Amy.

It is important to have end of life conversations even when you are young, and you are healthy. Amy and I had some time to talk about this and get deeply into it. My biggest question was how I could go on as a single parent after her. Those conversations led to her assuring me that I could do it and that I had a great relationship with each of our kids. We talked about Amy's service and what she wanted, we talked about practical things, financial issues, and just life issues I was about to face without her. We also talked about the fractured relationships with people we would have liked to repair and did.

Exhibit kindness to someone grieving. There's very little you can say that would be the "wrong" thing to say, so just reach out to someone you care about and say, "I am here, I am thinking about you." That goes such a long way. "Let's go out for a drink, it will put your mind to ease, or let's go out for a walk" puts the onus on the person who is grieving. It is like an empty promise. Try instead, "6:00 PM I get off work, I will drive by to see if you are up for a gentle walk. If not, I totally understand." In my own case, I was lucky to have a beautiful and loving community. I think we can do beautiful things in small doses that don't require a lot of effort but goes a long way in making someone feel better.

The words cancer and cancel look similar. Even though we had to cancel many of our plans as empty nesters, I was given the opportunity through this cancer experience to rediscover myself in many ways. You are intricately connected to someone else and then you are not. So, there you are. I have filled the intentional empty space that Amy left me with.....with meaning. Some people call it happiness, others call it joy. I think it is more being purposeful or meaningful.

I speak all over the world on topics like this and I commissioned a piece of art in her honor, as it is important to me. I adjusted my work life a lot to find meaning. I incorporated mindfulness and meditation in my life. I did learn a lot about myself, the Jason, in a world without his Amy.

The surprising thing for me to discover was the amazing ability of human beings to be resilient. For those first months (or years) the grief is way too overwhelming to even think about moving forward. Even baby steps are hard to take, but you'd be surprised at the incredible power of time. You have two choices…go to a bar and bury yourself in a bottle of whiskey or to emerge and move forward with that resilience that is in there. Every day I try to infuse my life with more meaning, more purpose and appreciating the fact that life is short, you never know what is next. For those of us that have gone through the depths of loss and grief, we have a different lens for life because we have been way down to the depths of despair. It is ok to experience anxiety and grief. But I promise to you, this will end at some point, and you will get back to experiencing joy and beauty and all the good things that come in life. Try each day to think of one thing you feel grateful for, and I promise you, you will find something. Enjoy the unexpected time you get with the ones you love.

Jason B. Rosenthal is a TED Speaker and the number one New York Times bestselling author of Dear Boy, cowritten with his daughter, Paris. He is also the subject of an essay written by his wife, Amy Krouse Rosenthal, called You May Want to Marry My Husband that went viral and was read by millions of readers worldwide. When his bride died of ovarian cancer after 26 years of marriage, Jason got in touch with real pain. He immediately reevaluated his life's work. Now, he speaks publicly and writes about issues related to processing grief and finding hope and joy amongst the pain.

# Life or something like it. Ovarcoming and the never ending spirit of it!

Allow me to take you to a room – imagine it being dark and silent with a few machines humming, loved ones encircling, and a life slowly fading. Sitting in one corner of that room several years ago, I watched my Mom breathe her last. It was the moment that the true spirit of Ovarcoming came into me. 'Ovarcoming' changed my life. I hope, in the reading of this book, it changed yours as well.

Let me take you back a few years, to 2009. Life was humming along. I had a great career and good friends, and by now I was Mom to the spunkiest 3-year-old on this planet. Then one day my dad called. He said, "Your Mom has ovarian cancer. Doctors are saying it is an advanced stage, and there's no hope of Ovarcoming". In that instant, my life as I knew it, fell apart – but at that time I didn't realize it was going to be an opportunity to rebuild myself in ways that I always wanted my life to be.

What followed in the next 11 months was a roller coaster of challenges, hope, prayers and acceptance. Mom's health began to decline after a few months.

I purchased my ticket to go visit her over Valentine's Day. Events took an unexpected turn - after 11 months of gracefully facing ovarian cancer, my beloved mother passed away. She was the rock of my life. We had a connection of lifetimes.

After her death, I struggled to embrace the peace of mind that comes with knowing it is over - that we have reached the end of the road. I had to keep her spirit and her legacy alive. I decided to leave my corporate career and create Ovarcome that has since then helped millions of women and families worldwide with awareness, education, and support. It was created to gift the spirit of Ovarcoming to all women diagnosed with ovarian cancer.

I flew to visit my Mom as many times as I could. Just sat there holding her hand, watched movies together, made dinner for her that oftentimes she couldn't eat, or just listened as she talked about her childhood, her first love, my dad, and her afterlife.

I realized that we as Caregivers give an incredible gift to those we care for. Keep giving this gift - because for you, someone still hopes, someone still fights, and someone still Ovarcomes.

Life begins on the other side of despair. The pressure to be happy is real – but we can't achieve it by avoiding sadness. Even during despair, there is always that ONE thing that is "right" in our lives. Let's fill our hearts with it. And let's never forget humor.

It's like when your therapist says that the best way to achieve true inner peace is to finish what you start and you have finished two bars of chocolate and feeling better already!

When my Mom was in the final stages of battling her cancer, she delved into self-introspection. She took time to understand what mattered to her most. She realized welcoming death plugged into machines was not how she wanted to cross the bridge.

She told us to take off all switches and plugs, declined visit requests that were not meaningful to her, and reminded her nurse when she brought with her a report with Mom's age mentioned wrong - "I may be dying, but I am not 85!" Humor stayed with her until the end.

We talked about her death – she worried about my life and Dad's life after she was gone. I reassured her that our lives would go on – I assured her that we would Ovarcome. Mom then told me "I want to Ovarcome life. I no longer want to fight a battle; I want to experience the freedom of surrender."

I promised her that I would sign all the release forms so she may choose her ending, so she could Ovarcome.

Through my journey, I have realized all our lives we drive ourselves to Ovarcome – to win the fight, to wage a war of hope, to triumph over challenges, to defeat and to prevail.

The act of Ovarcoming is not just to win. It is also to embrace reality. It's just as much about fighting as it is about giving up when it feels right.

Now I have 2 boys, and I tell them every day to practice gratitude and to live their best life by Ovarcoming the fear of not being able to Ovarcome. Because there is no such thing. Ovarcoming is not complicated – by doing what we can and by daring to believe in the silver lining in despair, we can Ovarcome. Ovarcoming is not a battle against losing - Ovarcoming is a deliberate journey of choosing.

**Keep Ovarcoming!**

**With love & gratitude always,**

**Runsi**
*Founder, Ovarcome*

**Keep the quiet light of Ovarcoming burning in your heart**

## The final chapter:
### Facing life with hope and purpose

It took one day to hear the words "you have cancer". It takes every day, to Ovarcome. Through the struggles and the challenges this journey brings, we realize how strong we can be, and how love, and the spirit of Ovarcoming can be a guiding light in the darkness.

It is hard to navigate a cancer diagnosis, but living every day with hope and as a gift will give you the strength and the peace you seek.

Your loved ones are there to surround you with love and light. They will stand by you in your pain and hope alongside with you as you heal.

Give yourself grace and love yourself - a lot. Reflect on what has been meaningful in your life. Allow yourself the heartache when it comes, immerse yourself in the waves of sadness if you must – but take time to focus on what is right in your life.

There is something that is right in all our lives. Find it. Fill your heart with it.

Embrace the simple acts of joy. Turn on your favorite song, connect with your favorite friend, visit your loved ones, write a blog, sweeten your coffee just an extra bit, be kind to a stranger, return the smile of a child at the grocery store, play with your pet, don't do laundry, break the routine, call your special person unscheduled – the list goes on.

Allow yourself happiness. Cherish your close relationships. After you have experienced the brutality of a day filled with treatment, hug your child, grandchild or fur child and feel that magical wave of love and happiness surrounding you. Don't deny yourself the love that you know exists.

Indulge in simple pleasures, express gratitude, keep the faith, recognize your blessings, and always believe in miracles.

In this path of Ovarcoming, each story is unique, and every experience is singular. Through its twists and turns however, each path leads to the realization that we are not alone and that there's a hope that's bigger than we are.

In this final chapter, may you find the hope to give meaning to every moment of your life and the promise to carry it forward. As this book ends, may the purpose of hope begin.

Find this hope and embrace the spirit of Ovarcoming - today and every day.

# Acknowledgments

Cancer is isolating, but the journey of Ovarcoming doesn't have to be.

In walking this path together, we are eternally grateful to all our Ovarcomers that have shared their stories, the ups and downs of their journeys, their inspiration, and their indomitable spirit to Ovarcome.

We are thankful to all Caregivers that have shared through their own stories, what it means to stand by their loved ones with unwavering love and commitment as they travel the road to Ovarcoming, together.

We are thankful to all Physicians, Researchers, Nurses, Social Workers, Counselors, and Support Staff – all Healthcare Heroes that give their best each day to enhance and improve the lives of all Ovarcomers as they walk this path of Ovarcoming.

We thank all fellow cancer organizations, and all our partners that work tirelessly each day to bring new answers, new programs, and new solutions to our community.

We thank our Board, our staff, and our volunteers – this book of inspiration wouldn't have been possible without the dedication of their incredible commitment, that is the driving force behind our ability to create meaningful impact and improve lives touched by cancer.

To everyone that has stood by us, for a minute or for miles beyond – thank you.

Together, We Ovarcome.

This book is a work of creative nonfiction. While all stories depicted in this book of inspiration are true and based on real life experiences, some names and identifying details may have been modified for storytelling purposes.

www.ingramcontent.com/pod-product-compliance
Lightning Source LLC
Chambersburg PA
CBHW032100090426
42743CB00007B/188